How to Mom

HOW TO MOM

Carol Boswell, Ron Barrett, and Dale Burg

A JOHN BOSWELL ASSOCIATES BOOK

A DELL TRADE PAPERBACK

A DELL TRADE PAPERBACK
Published by
Dell Publishing
a division of
Bantam Doubleday Dell Publishing Group, Inc.
1540 Broadway
New York, New York 10036

Library of Congress Cataloging-in-Publication Data
Boswell, Carol, 1945–
        How to mom / Carol Boswell, Ron Barrett, and Dale Burg.
          p.   cm.
        ISBN 0-440-50656-5
        1. Motherhood—Miscellanea. 2. Mother and child—Miscellanea. 3. Creative activities and seat work. I. Barrett, Ron. II. Burg, Dale. III. Title.
        HQ769.B73   1995
        306.874'3—dc20   94-42032
                                                       CIP

Designed by Ron Barrett

Typeset by Jackson Typesetting

Printed in the United States of America

Published simultaneously in Canada.

May 1995

10 9 8 7 6 5 4 3 2 1

To our moms,
Matty, Lillian and Miriam,
who have two and a half centuries
of wisdom among them

ACKNOWLEDGMENTS

The Authors gratefully acknowledge the following individuals for their support: John Boswell, Patty Brown, Ward Calhoun, Kristen Kiser, Dick Nusser and Leslie Schnur.

Thanks also to Becky and Jessica Barrett, Harriet Bell, Beverly Hill, Sylvia Khan, Phillip McLemore, the Manhattan Ballet School, Christopher Pisacane, Anne Roche and Barbara Schubeck.

CONTENTS

Introduction

Insanity is hereditary. You can get it from your kids.—Sam Levenson

Name a human experience that is simultaneously terrifying and exhilarating; potentially frustrating but wildly fulfilling; capable of plunging you to the lowest depths and buoying you to the loftiest heights. Other than bungee jumping, that is.

What we're thinking about here is being a mom.

Despite the enormous responsibility the title implies, there are no licenses required, no courses to prepare you, no qualifying test to pass. All you need to be a mom is a child. And the minute you have one, you're expected to settle right into the job, which pretty much boils down to keeping civilization going.

This involves carrying out—and by example, teaching—a variety of skills that generally fall into one of three categories.

The nurturing skills: Such as making chicken soup. Caring for the pets. Leading the cheers.

The survival skills. Including patching a boo-boo. Growing a windowsill farm. Finding a bargain.

And the skills that tradition dictates. While the particulars vary widely from cultural group to cultural group, these are carefully observed, since they are what each believes sets them apart from species that are furred, feathered, and scaly. In Western society, these skills include setting the table, dressing for the relatives, and writing thank-you notes.

While nurturing and survival skills seem to go without saying, the traditional skills often prompt children to ask, with their charming though maddening insightfulness, "Do we have to?" A successful mom sticks by her guns and convinces her child that the answer is "Yes," even when she herself is not quite sure why. (For example, it is hard to build a really solid case for making a bed.)

The good news is that, once launched into Momdom, you will undoubtedly discover that you have a darn good idea about how to proceed. Some of it is innate. Much of it you may remember from what your own mom did.

But in case you've forgotten a trick or two, this book is here to help you.

And if at times being a mom drives you to the edge of insanity—well, part of insanity, of course, is mad and irrational joy. And that is what being a mom brings you, in spades.

—Carol Boswell, Ron Barrett, and Dale Burg

How to Jump Rope

One rope is all the equipment your child needs to have some fun along with what we have recently discovered is aerobic exercise. Add two people to turn the rope, plus one or more additional jumpers, and your children have the ingredients for hours of entertainment. Of the many variations on basic rope-jumping, here are just a few.

SOLO JUMPING

The easiest type is the double jump: jump once to let the rope pass under your feet and a second time when the rope is at its highest overhead point. Turning the rope very fast and jumping only once as it passes below your feet—like a boxer in training—is harder.

"Crossing over" is a feat for the experienced jumper. It involves crossing the hand while the rope is turning and requires terrific eye/hand/foot coordination.

JUMP VARIATIONS

Hop instead of jump.
High jump. The rope goes around twice while you are still in the air.

JUMP CHALLENGES

Jump and bounce a ball at the same time.
Put a marker (a stone or stick) on the ground as you jump, pick it up on your next jump, put it down again on the next jump, and so on—until you miss.
Jump and count from 1 to 12, making a quarter turn clockwise each time.

RHYMES AND GAMES FOR JUMPING

All kinds of candy in the dish,
How many pieces do you wish?
1-2-3-4-etc.

Rope turners continue turning and counting until jumper misses.

Policeman, policeman, do your duty;
Here comes [jumper's name], she's a cutie.
She can jump. She can twist.
But I bet she can't do this.

Jumper invents a stunt, then jumps out and lets next person go. Variation: next jumper imitates this stunt, then does her own.

A my name is *Annie*
And my husband's name is *Arnold*
We come from *Alabama*
And we grow *asparagus*.

First jumper does the A words, then jumps out, next one in uses the same chant but substitutes words starting with B, and so on through the alphabet. The jumper is eliminated who "blanks out" on any word. The winner is the last one to remain in the game.

ROPE-TURNING VARIATIONS

■ **Rock the cradle.** Rope is rocked back and forth rather than being turned.

■ **Double dutch:** Use two ropes or one very long rope (which passes behind the back of one of the turners). Turn the ropes toward each other slowly—like an egg beater.

■ **Hot Pepper:** Turn the rope *very* fast.

How to Dress for the Cold, the Heat, and the Relatives

Moms, being sensitive both barometrically and socially, always know the right thing to wear for any time and occasion—from a trip to Antartica to a visit to Aunt Anne.

DRESSING FOR THE COLD

A sweater is a garment a child wears when his or her mother feels cold, no matter what the season. Strangely, children themselves are unlikely to acknowledge the cold except at times when it is exceedingly inconvenient for example, just as you have settled yourself into a prime viewing location to watch the Thanksgiving Parade. Frequently you have to wait until the child's skin has acquired a bluish pallor to know that the child is, indeed, cold.

In the coldest weather, children too young to protest are usually bundled into a one-piece snowsuit. The test of a snowsuit's protective value is how effectively it renders a child immobile. Thus a child dressed in a top-of-the-line snowsuit assumes the spread-eagle position that you may recognize from the Leonardo da Vinci drawing and could, at least

in theory, be rolled like a hoop through the snow. The extremities are protected with mittens and booties. Until the child is walking these latter items are virtually interchangeable.

Mittens are warmer than gloves, and in very cold weather two pairs are better than one. Consider yourself lucky if you can find any.

THE TWO STAGES
OF DRESSING
IN CHILDHOOD

1. DIAPERS

2. WHAT THE OTHER
KIDS ARE WEARING

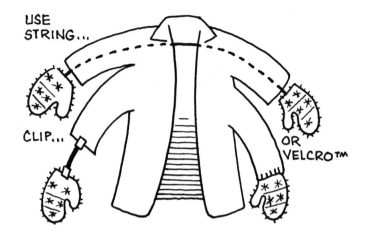

USE STRING...

CLIP...

OR VELCRO™

REMOVE CARROTS FROM BAGS BEFORE PLACING OVER CHILD'S FOOT

One way to keep track of a young child's mittens is by attaching them to each other with a long string, then running the string through the snowsuit. (To be on the very safe side, attach another end of the string to mother.) Or attach them with Velcro™ to cuffs. With an older child, glove loss is an unavoidable fact of life. Though you may be tempted to glue mittens to your child's hands, this is not recommended.

The transition from snowsuit to two-piece snowsuit or heavy jacket and jeans is usually made shortly after a child graduates from diapers and you have had one or two opportunities to suit down a youngster who expresses an urgent need for a bathroom visit just as you've spent ten minutes suiting her up.

Putting boots on your child is less likely to be a prechiropractic situation if you slip a plastic bag over your child's foot, then slip the bag into a boot. Older children will insist that sneakers, which they generally consider the all-occasion shoe (see **Dressing for the Relatives**), are perfectly adequate substitutes for boots.

DRESSING FOR THE HEAT

Getting children to dress down is rarely a problem. What is a problem is convincing them to cover all exposed areas with sunscreen, which they consider yucky. Stay firm.

Savvy camp directors know that one way to dispose you favorably toward their camp is to assure you that their counselors supervise sunscreen application. Unless you know that the counselor's mothers will be on hand to remind the counselors themselves about sunscreen, don't count on it.

YOU MISSED HIS LEFT ELBOW.

CAMP NOLAKE

CAMP NOLAKE STAFF

CHILDREN'S DRESS CODE (BOY)

FORMAL

← CAP WORN SIDEWAYS

T-SHIRT

ONE SHOE UNLACED

INFORMAL

← CAP WORN BACKWARDS

T-SHIRT

TWO SHOES UNLACED

DRESSING FOR THE RELATIVES

Very young girls often have no problem with "dressing up" and in fact may even wear a tiara to breakfast. But many older children act as if wearing anything other than jeans or sweatsuits is as unbearable as walking around all day in pantyhose that are the wrong size. Even if you win the dress/skirt/jacket/tie skirmishes and your child has agreed to forsake the baseball cap, you will still have the sneakers bridge to cross. Fortunately, standards have lowered just about everywhere today. Most of the time, as Cole Porter said—though even *he* had no idea to what extent this would be true—"anything goes."

However, whether anything goes with everything is another matter. One simple rule of thumb is to say that if two items of two different colors are being worn, a third garment must match either one color or the other. The issue of pattern mixing is more complex. Though the Duke of Windsor pioneered pattern-on-pattern dressing, and some of the fringe fashion designers have mastered this look, few adults—and still fewer children—have quite the same knack. On the smallest child you can pin a button saying, "I dressed myself today." The bad taste of older children will pale beside the other, larger issues they will present.

A BROKEN RULE OF THUMB

Lost Mom Arts

Among the skills that moms are no longer expected to pass on:

■ How to skin a mastodon

■ How to make corn meal

■ How to weave on a loom

■ How to dance the minuet

■ How to cinch a corset

■ How to faint

■ How to embroider a sampler

■ How to churn butter

■ How to card wool

■ How to use a hat pin

■ How to play canasta

■ How to make Welsh rarebit (except if you're Welsh)

■ How to use a compact

■ How to make a mustard plaster

■ How to tie-dye

■ How to iron hair

13

How to Pack a Lunch Box

What the attaché case is to the newly minted M.B.A. or J.D., the lunch box is to the young child who is setting off for a full-day school or camp for the first time. Just as an adult ponders whether to choose black or burgundy, soft-sided or hard, your child will have a similarly delicious dilemma. Will it be the plush-toy purple lunch box or the dinosaur green? The princess or the pony? The lady or the tiger? And, like the adult who may tote only a pair of gym shorts in the brand-new case, your child will be focused much more on the status quality of this accessory than on what goes inside. That remains mom's concern.

The ideal box-lunch items are not only good for the child but also *items that the child will actually eat,* a point that should not get lost in the shuffle. The tuna fish, carrot sticks, and raisins lose all their nutritional benefits if they are never transferred from the lunch box to the stomach of the child. Furthermore, it is discouraging when a box so optimistically and lovingly packed in the morning returns in the evening with its contents intact and probably salmonella-laced. (Of course, an empty lunch box is no guarantee of anything. Your child may have simply traded whatever was in there for a handful of corn chips. But there is no point dwelling on such thoughts.)

Appealing to the child's intellect is generally futile. Such notions as "food groups," "well-balanced," and "food pyramids" (see chart) remain elusive until adulthood and in many cases, straight on through it. If you prefer to move out of the peanut-butter-and-jelly rut, you are more likely to have success if you think of foods that are crunchy, that are fun to eat with the fingers, and/or that come in unusual packaging. And be sure to keep perishables safe by putting into the lunch box a cold-pack or a container of yogurt or box of juice that has been frozen. (Bonus: the juice and yogurt will thaw out and can be consumed at lunchtime.)

Things to Put in the Lunch Box Other than Sandwiches

- Air-popped popcorn
- Raw vegetables with salad dressing
- Small boiled potatoes or pretzel sticks with cheese dip*
- Fruit slices with a container of yogurt for dipping
- Breadsticks with ham wrapped around them
- Kabobs of vegetables, fruit, and/or cheese
- Celery stuffed with cheese spread or peanut butter
- Cored apple or pear stuffed with peanut butter
- String cheese
- Individual containers of applesauce, canned fruit, or pudding (don't forget the spoon)
- Hard-boiled eggs
- Chicken leg
- Napkin
- Mint
- Note or drawing from mom

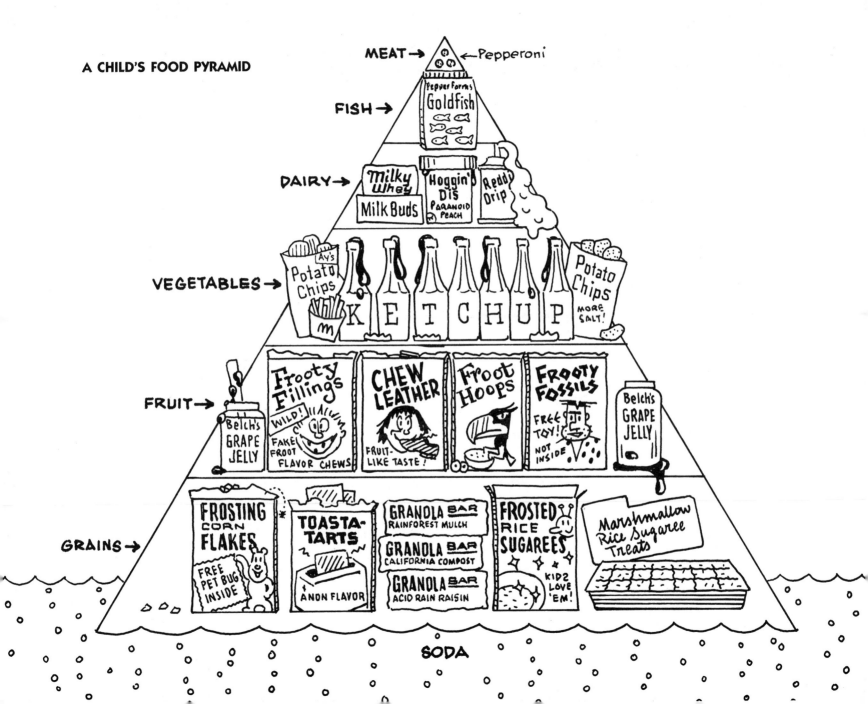

How to Plait a Braid

Braiding is much less complicated than hooking up a VCR. Also, unlike the VCR instructions, these directions have not been translated from a foreign tongue and there is no way you can give yourself an electric shock if you happen to make a mistake on your first try.

Soon you will find braiding so easy that you (and your daughter) will be able to do it in your sleep, which will come in handy on many mornings. The essential requirements are medium to long hair that has been combed free of tangles, a couple of elastic bands, and some patience.

TWO BRAIDS
The classic, Dorothy-in-the-Wizard-of-Oz variety.

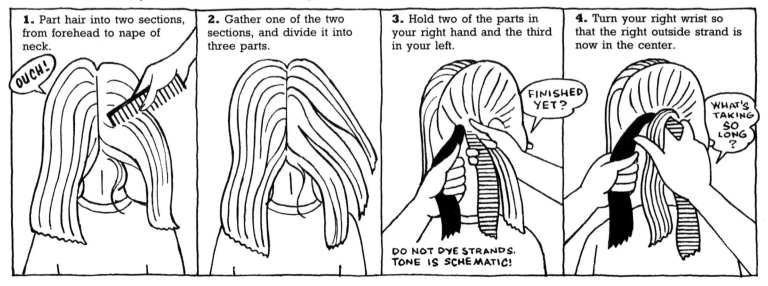

1. Part hair into two sections, from forehead to nape of neck.

2. Gather one of the two sections, and divide it into three parts.

3. Hold two of the parts in your right hand and the third in your left.

4. Turn your right wrist so that the right outside strand is now in the center.

5. With your left hand, grasp that center strand. You are now holding two strands in your left hand, one in your right.

6. Turn your left wrist so that the left outside strand has crossed over into the center.

7. Take the center strand into the right hand.

8. Repeat all these instructions starting from step 4, and keep going until you come to the end.
Use an elastic band to hold the braid in place.

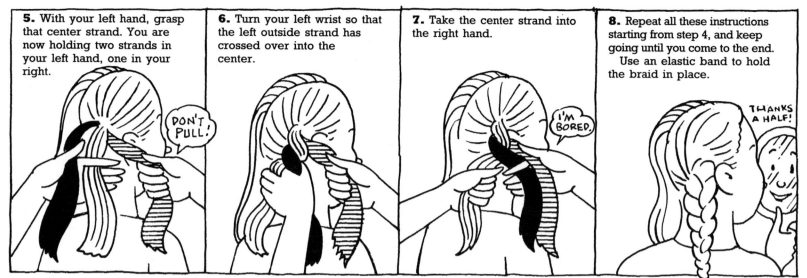

SINGLE BRAID

Gather all the hair into a ponytail and use an elastic band to hold it in place. Then divide the ponytail into three parts. Continue from step 3 above.

FRENCH BRAID

A French braid starts higher up, and you add sections of hair as you work.

1. Find the highest point of the crown of the head. Gather a section of hair that goes from there to about two inches behind the hairline—at the point where bangs usually begin.

2. Divide the section into three strands. Cross the right and then the left over the center, as for a basic braid.

3. Hold all three strands in your left hand. Pull a small section of hair back from the right side of the face and add it to the right strand.

4. Pull the center strand all the way to the right. Move all hair to your right hand. As you work, constantly pull the hairs tighter.

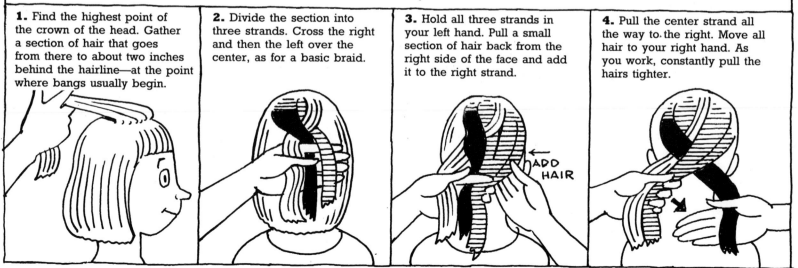

5. Add more hair to the left strand, keeping hands close to the head. Pull the center strand all the way to the left

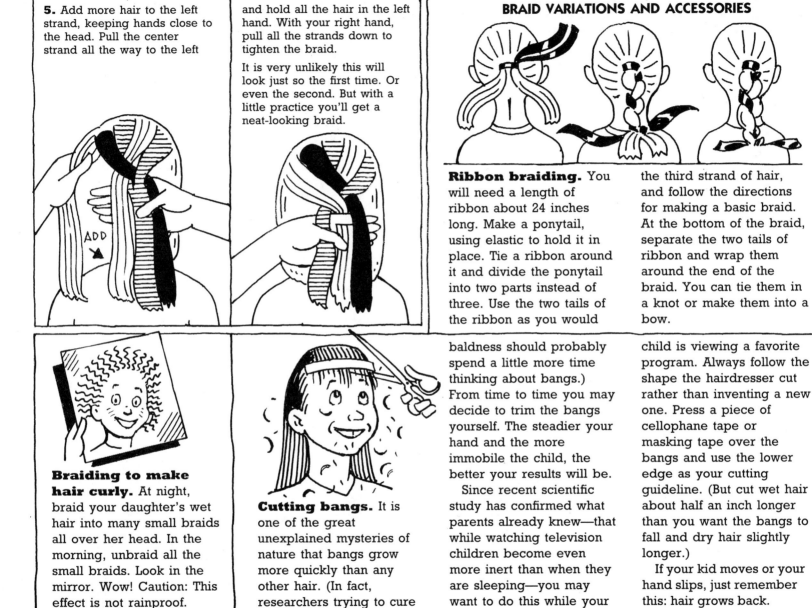

ADD

and hold all the hair in the left hand. With your right hand, pull all the strands down to tighten the braid.

It is very unlikely this will look just so the first time. Or even the second. But with a little practice you'll get a neat-looking braid.

Braiding to make hair curly. At night, braid your daughter's wet hair into many small braids all over her head. In the morning, unbraid all the small braids. Look in the mirror. Wow! Caution: This effect is not rainproof.

Cutting bangs. It is one of the great unexplained mysteries of nature that bangs grow more quickly than any other hair. (In fact, researchers trying to cure

BRAID VARIATIONS AND ACCESSORIES

Ribbon braiding. You will need a length of ribbon about 24 inches long. Make a ponytail, using elastic to hold it in place. Tie a ribbon around it and divide the ponytail into two parts instead of three. Use the two tails of the ribbon as you would the third strand of hair, and follow the directions for making a basic braid. At the bottom of the braid, separate the two tails of ribbon and wrap them around the end of the braid. You can tie them in a knot or make them into a bow.

baldness should probably spend a little more time thinking about bangs.) From time to time you may decide to trim the bangs yourself. The steadier your hand and the more immobile the child, the better your results will be.

Since recent scientific study has confirmed what parents already knew—that while watching television children become even more inert than when they are sleeping—you may want to do this while your child is viewing a favorite program. Always follow the shape the hairdresser cut rather than inventing a new one. Press a piece of cellophane tape or masking tape over the bangs and use the lower edge as your cutting guideline. (But cut wet hair about half an inch longer than you want the bangs to fall and dry hair slightly longer.)

If your kid moves or your hand slips, just remember this: hair grows back.

H--w t-- Fix a B--o-B--o

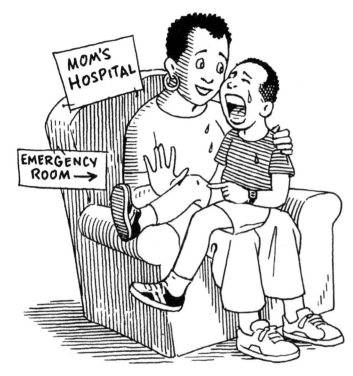

MOM'S HOSPITAL

EMERGENCY ROOM →

Even moms who daydreamed through health class will occasionally be called on to administer first aid. For serious medical advice, of course, the services of a trustworthy pediatrician are essential, but many minor problems are easily handled by even the nonscientifically inclined. And fortunately, the most effective child-healing equipment is easy to administer and always available: a lap to sit the child in, arms to hold the child, and soothing words of comfort. Here are some other basic procedures.

S-S-S-S-S   S-S-S-S-S

TAKING A TEMPERATURE WITHOUT A THERMOMETER

This is one of the most mythic of mothering skills, developed postpartum and over time. Mothers of infants must still rely on calibrated instruments but by the time your child has reached toddlerhood, you will probably be able to use the hand or lip method with sufficient accuracy to determine whether a child is well enough to go to school. However, if the illness seems serious enough to consult your doctor, stick with the calibrated instrument.

Hand method: Apply back of hand briefly to child's forehead. A child who has a temperature will feel hot to the touch. If the reading is inconclusive, take back-of-hand readings on cheeks and nape of neck.

Lip method: Place your lips against child's forehead for about ten seconds. If the forehead initially feels warm but gradually meets the temperature of your lips, the child probably does not have a fever. If the surrounding forehead remains comparatively warm, the child may have a fever.

GETTING THE MEDICINE DOWN

Despite many dramatic advances in the field of medicine, the folks at the pharmaceutical companies have yet to lick the problem of bad-tasting and difficult-to-swallow medications. So have your child suck on an ice cube or frozen popsickle to numb taste buds immediately prior to taking bad-tasting medicine. And help a pill go down easily by administering it in a teaspoon of applesauce or pudding.

RELIEVING AN ITCH

As most people discover, the best thing to do for an itch is to scratch it. But the itch from a bug bite can be very persistent. Remedies include smothering, freezing, heating, or numbing the problem area.

You can paint on clear nailpolish. You can rub on vinegar or rubbing alcohol. Or you may apply buttermilk, plain yogurt, or a paste of baking soda with water.

TREATING MINOR WOUNDS

Though the sight of blood in and of itself may not be upsetting, the sight of one's *own* blood generally is. Take a tip from one of nature's wonderful notions—camouflage—and keep a red washcloth in your bathroom specifically reserved to clean up minor wounds. Skip the creams, ointments, and so on; Mother Nature does the best job of healing. Just clean the area with soap and water and put a bandage on top for protection and as a badge of courage.

SOOTHING A BUMP

Ice packs relieve pain and reduce the chance of swelling, but best of all, they serve as a distraction, especially if the cold comfort turns out to be a surprise: a bag of frozen peas, for example, makes a fine ice pack. For a small

COLD
COMFORT

wound, mom can produce a packet of mustard or duck sauce from the Chinese restaurant tucked away in the freezer for just such a purpose. Or offer an ice pop both as consolation and comfort for a bruised lip.

EXTRACTING A SPLINTER

The grisly custom of using a needle to remove a splinter, according to current thinking, causes more infections than it prevents. If you

paint a little rubber cement or household glue over the area where the splinter is located, wait for it to dry, and then peel it off, the splinter will often come along with it. Glass splinters require professional assistance.

REMOVING A BANDAGE

If you let the child pull the bandage off, it will hurt less than if you pull it off. Coat the bandage with salad oil or baby oil and it'll come off easier. Better yet, wait until the bandage falls off of its own free will.

How to Make Chicken Soup

Even the doctors who won't go on record to say so will acknowledge privately that chicken soup can cure the common cold along with a host of other maladies.

The only ingredient you definitely need for chicken soup is chicken. (Rattlesnake, rabbit, frog legs, and other meats that reputedly taste just like chicken may not produce the same results.)

Many cultures have their own recipes for chicken soup, but all of them start with the basic recipe.

BASIC CHICKEN SOUP

Fowl, which is older and tougher, makes a richer broth. But you can use any kind of chicken, even one that is labeled broiler or roaster and whether or not it is whole or cut into pieces. (If cut into pieces, it may be easier to fit into a pot).

Ingredients

3½- to 4-pound chicken makes a nice amount of soup

All of the following are optional:
1 teaspoon salt
½ teaspoon pepper
2 teaspoons lemon juice
4 minced garlic cloves
1 teaspoon dill weed
1 medium peeled onion
2 medium peeled carrots
2 medium stalks celery
Contents of bag sold in supermarket as "soup greens"

1. Unwrap the chicken from the plastic and reach inside to remove the paper bag that contains the kidneys, heart, and liver. Reach inside the other end and take out the neck. Cook those parts for the cat or give them to someone who knows how to make gravy. Or throw them out.

I'M GOIN' IN!

2. Put the chicken into the pot and add enough water to cover (about 12 cupfuls) along with any of the optional ingredients that appeal to you.

3. Cover the pot and cook on low heat—enough to keep the broth simmering—for about 50 minutes or until you can easily push a fork through the meat and the dark meat is not pink. (Fowl may take 90 minutes or more to cook.)

4. Pour liquid through a colander or strainer into another pot. This liquid is the broth, or stock. Put it into the refrigerator and when it is cold, lift the fat off the top.

5. Discard the limp, cooked vegetables that remain in the colander. Remove skin and bones from the meat. Shred any larger hunks of meat into bite-sized pieces.

When you want to eat the chicken soup, heat the broth along with any or all of the following: cooked noodles, cooked carrots, and—if you want to blaze new paths in chicken-soup territory—other vegetables. Or use the broth to make chicken soup with a foreign flavor.

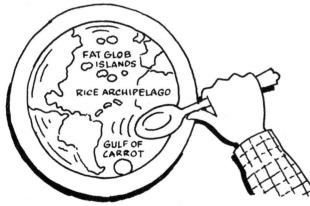

CHICKEN SOUP AROUND THE WORLD

- **Welch Chicken Soup (Cock-A-Leekie):** contains barley, leeks, and cream

- **Greek Chicken Soup (Avgolemono):** contains lemon and eggs

- **Spanish Chicken Soup:** contains onion, garlic, rice, and chorizo (sausage)

- **Italian Chicken Soup (Straciatella):** contains eggs and spinach, topped with Parmesan cheese

- **Indian Chicken Soup (Mulligatawny):** contains apple, ginger, cumin, and yogurt

- **Chinese Chicken Soup (Won Ton):** contains strips of pork and noodle dumplings

- **Bubba Goldberg's Chicken Soup:** chicken feet are added at beginning, then discarded; may contain matzoh balls.

OTHER HEALING FOOD AND DRINK

When your child has a fever
- Ginger ale, cola drinks, and other sodas
- Sports drinks
- Gelatin dessert (either before or after it has gelled)
- Chipped ice

When your child has an upset stomach
- Bananas
- Rice
- Applesauce
- Toast
- Peppermint or chamomile tea (what Peter Rabbit's mother gave him)
- Plus anything that's okay to eat when you have a fever

When your child needs comforting
- Chocolate treats (see pp. 35–37)
- Macaroni and cheese
- Mashed potatoes

How to Write a Thank-You Note

Since the invention of the telephone, some people consider writing a thank-you note as outdated as adding with a pencil instead of a computer. However, grandmothers and a surprising number of other relatives are not part of this group. They consider a thank-you note a sign of good breeding, proof that a child has made some effort to compensate for the giver's expense and efforts, and an attractive adornment for the refrigerator.

THINGS TO REMEMBER

A thank-you note can be short.

It does not have to be terribly creative.

And it need not even be sincere.

Thanks.
I love it.

In fact, teaching your child to write an acceptable thank-you note even for a hated gift is good preparation for a diplomatic career, in case your child wants one.

BASIC THANK-YOU NOTE

First sentence. This is the easy one. "Thank you for the [adjective] [name of item]." The adjective can be neutral ("nice") or specific ("blue").

Second sentence. Add a detail about the gift. For example:

Tell where you used the gift and when. "I took it to the park yesterday."

Tell how you used it. "My friends and I played with it."

Tell what you especially liked about it. "It's

24

my favorite color." "I always wanted one."

If the gift is money, tell what you plan to do with it. "I will spend it to buy ——."

Small children may wish to draw a picture of themselves playing with or wearing the present.

If you can't think of a single nice thing to say about the gift, you can just say, "It was nice of you to send it."

Third sentence. An older child may be expected to add additional information about the present or about the birthday party or holiday celebration at which it was received. For example:

If it's a birthday present, tell where your party was held. Or say how many friends were there. Or tell whatever special thing you did for your birthday.

If it's a Christmas present, write something about what you did over the holidays. Or just say you will be sad when the holidays end.

Fourth sentence. Close. Here are two all-purpose sentences.

"I hope I see you soon."
"Thank you again."

REASONS YOUR CHILD SHOULD WRITE A THANK-YOU NOTE

■ It is polite to write a thank-you note.
■ A thank-you note makes the person who gave the present feel good.
■ If you want a present next year, you had better write a thank-you note this year.

How to Find a Bargain

Although little girls seem more predisposed to shop than little boys, with the right attitude or reward, you can make this skill appealing to both sexes.

DEFINING A BARGAIN

There are two criteria in determining whether something is a "bargain." (1) *Cost:* It should be inexpensive, or less expensive than an identical or similar item. (2) *Utility:* It should be something that you can use. It is important to practice shopping at odd-lot warehouses and army-navy stores to learn how to avoid items that meet criteria (1) but not (2).

PROSPECTING

Many sale or bargain items are "displayed" in large bins that you have to search through to find just the right size, color, or design. What is important to teach here is the proper attitude. The activity should not be seen as shopping but rather as prospecting, an experience akin to being an archeologist or prospector sifting through a dig. In this context, finding the right bathmat or pajama set becomes a challenge and potential thrill rather than a mundane chore.

BLOWOUT SALE!

CLOSEOUT!

SALE!

Sale! ANTI-LEECH GAITERS

A 12 CBR

GAS MASK TYPE A-12

MEETS CRITERIA 1 BUT NOT 2

BARGAIN DIG

PRE-PRE-SHRUNK PERIOD

MFR'S FAULT

POST-ORLON UPTHRUST

POLYESTERIAN FOSSILS

SALE

HAGGLING

In America, the custom is to put price tags on items. If you do not like the posted price, you take your business elsewhere. However, people who have been trained to shop in the bazaars of the Middle East or have had dealings with slick real estate operators or car dealers here at home know that many purchases are negotiable. Items that are soiled, have missing parts, or are otherwise imperfect but are good enough for your purpose may sometimes be bought at discount if you strike the right note between hautiness ("How could you presume to sell these discolored shoes at full price?") and obsequiousness ("It would be so gracious of you to reduce the cost of these sneakers that have yellowed in the window").

EXCHANGES AND RETURNS

What at first appears to be a bargain may upon reflection seem to be a big mistake. It is important to return or exchange any items about which you have second thoughts at the risk of raising the pro rata cost of other bargains. (Naturally, take into account the costs involved in the return or exchange: fuel, parking, tolls, and the cost of new bargains you may find.) Teach your child not to be intimidated by the prospect of insisting on a return or exchange. Retailing, after all, is built on the principle "The customer is always right," though some of the younger clerks may not know this.

PLACES TO AVOID IF YOU ARE LOOKING FOR BARGAINS
- Airport souvenir shops
- Hotel boutiques
- Stores with the word *Rue* in the title
- Places where the salespeople are dressed better than you are

- Tokyo

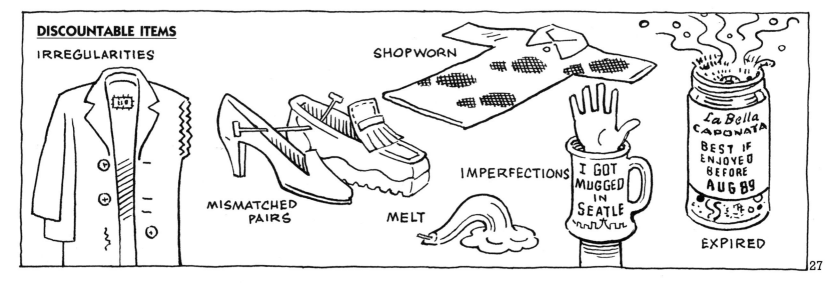

DISCOUNTABLE ITEMS

IRREGULARITIES

SHOPWORN

MISMATCHED PAIRS

MELT

IMPERFECTIONS

I GOT MUGGED IN SEATTLE

La Bella CAPONATA BEST IF ENJOYED BEFORE AUG 89

EXPIRED

How to Spend a Rainy Day

What kids today find most amazing about the story of Noah's Ark is how everyone spent forty days and nights indoors without a VCR. More than ever, it is important for mom to introduce children to pastimes that help them create fun on their own. Everyone will discover that it is surprisingly enjoyable to sit cozily inside, listening to the rainfall as you play a game, solve a puzzle, or work on a project like those suggested below. (Of course, it's also nice when the sun comes out again!)

MAKE PLAY CLAY

There's no need to Pay-Doh when you already have the ingredients in your kitchen for a fine play clay. With this all-purpose stuff-of-creation, your child can produce many items, including:

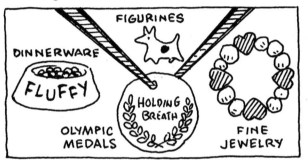

Though play clay will become quite hard, do not bake macaroni and cheese (or any other food) in a play clay casserole. The play clay will merge with your meal.

Ingredients

4 cups flour
1 cup salt
1½ cups water
Optional: 1 tbs. powdered alum (to retard spoilage)
  1 tbs. cooking oil (to make it softer)
  Food coloring

1. Mix dry ingredients.

2. Stir in water, oil, and a few drops of food coloring. When well mixed, knead the dough with your hands for about a minute to make it smooth.

Whatever play clay is not being used at the moment should be kept in a sealed plastic bag or covered bowl, since it dries in the air. Unused play clay will keep in the refrigerator for about a month (and should be brought to room temperature before play).

Medallions, pendants, tree ornaments.

Using a rolling pin or soda bottle, roll play clay to ½ inch thick on a floured board. If it's too sticky, add more flour. Cut the clay with a cookie cutter and punch a hole near the top (using a drinking straw) to pass a string or ribbon through. Let it air dry for a few days or bake at 250°F on a floured cookie sheet. It will take an hour or more, depending on thickness. Check with a toothpick to see if it's done. If it's getting too brown, cover it with foil, lower the temperature, and cook longer. It can be painted with acrylic paints.

Beads. Roll clay into balls big enough to be pushed onto a straw, leaving ½ inch between them. This is a bead kabob. Dry as above. Cut the beads off the straw and paint. String them on yarn, tie the ends, and get ready for glamour.

Decorative bowl. Mold from a lump or build of coils. Pasta can be pressed into its side before it dries.

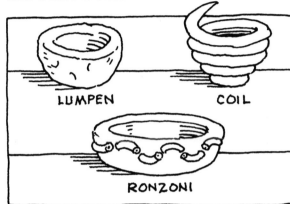

LUMPEN   COIL

RONZONI

BAKE AND COOK
See **How to Make Chocolate Treats**, pp. 35–37.

PLAY WORD GAMES
See **How to Take a Car Trip That Doesn't Drive You Crazy**, pp. 50–51.

OTHER GAMES THAT MOMS CAN PLAY
- Pickup sticks
- Jacks
- Candyland, Chutes and Ladders, Sorry, Go to the Head of the Class, Monopoly, Clue, and other board games
- Checkers
- Old Maid, Go Fish, War, and other card games
- Simon Says

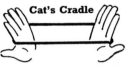

Cat's Cradle

1. Loop string around all fingers except thumb.

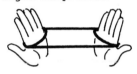

2. Loop it again, this time so it crosses palms.

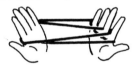

3. Use right middle finger to catch string running across left palm. Pull hands apart.

4. Repeat Step 3 with left middle finger snd string across right palm.

See neighborhood cat's cradle expert for advanced maneuvers.

PRODUCE A PUPPET THEATRE
See How to Put on a Puppet Show, pp. 84–85.

ACT OUT A FANTASY
See How to Make Believe, p. 91.

WEAVE A DAISY CHAIN
Take shelter beneath an umbrella and go outside to collect daisies or any abundant wildflower, such as clover, to make a crown, a necklace, or—for the short of patience—a bracelet. If you've noticed a great dissimilarity between your child and the innocents in Victorian children's books, you will find that daisy accessories are the great levelers.

Clover stems are flexible and tough enough so that slitting and clipping are unnecessary.

To make the chain, just knot the stem of one clover around the stem of the next. Tie off with the last stem.

Eco-wise moms will not, of course, deflower the countryside to produce flower accessories. They know how mad it makes the bees.

Projects Better Left to Arts and Crafts Counselors

- Lanyards
- Potholders
- Dried apple dolls
- Rag rugs from spools
- Wooden birdhouse
- Papier mâché
- Anything involving plaster of paris

1. When children pluck flowers they often bring up the entire root system, so use scissors instead. Leave a stem the length of a child's hand on each cut daisy.

2. With a butter knife, cut a slit through the stem about 1 inch from the bottom. Mom—*not* the child—should perform this step.

3. Insert a second daisy through the slit in the stem of the first. Pull until blossom is at the stem. Cut the second stem as you did the first and pull through a third flower.

4. Repeat until chain is desired length. Then use a paper clip to join the stem of the last daisy to the stem of the first.

ARM HOLE →

This enchanting floor-length sheath was cut from the top of an old sock. It's caught at the waist with a snippet of ribbon.

HEEL HOLE →

TOE HOLE

FASHION A DOLL DRESS

Stop paying high prices for big-name designer doll fashions for 14-inch dolls. Stop paying for blister packs and other packaging your child's doll can't wear.

Is this doll's full skirt bouffant with crinolines? No! It's a fluffy tissue wraparound with a wide, stylish cinch belt of masking tape.

Norma Kamali? Guess again! It's Norma KaDolly! Cut a head hole in the center of a facial tissue, add a pattern with markers and a yarn belt. Voilà! A dress you'd pay dollars for in the store.

Best of all, when the dress gets shabby, you can blow your nose in it.

31

How to Get Ready for School

Though there is no particular reason that mom should be the driving force who gets the family out the door in the morning while Dad reminds people to turn out the lights and is in charge of sports statistics, in many homes the division of labor runs along these lines. Probably this is true because moms seem better able to get everyone awakened, dressed, and breakfasted without confusing the child who should be carrying brownies for the bake sale with the one who should be wearing the Brownie uniform.

AWAKENING

As the military and most camp directors have discovered, it is quite efficient to use a bugle for reveille. At one blow you can rouse everyone in the family and half the neighborhood besides. So maybe it is not such a good idea to use a bugle. Though alarm clocks work for some, others would manage to sleep if Big Ben were gonging beneath the pillow. In any case, there is no substitute for a wake-up by mom.

Pulling up the shade or opening the blinds or curtains to let in the light of day sends a subliminal message to your sleeping child that it is time to get up. But what really starts the day off right is a wake-up kiss and maybe even a hug.

Turning on the radio may help, since periodic announcements that time is moving along may remind a child to do the same. And some children find it stimulating to start the

AWAKENING METHODS (FROM GENTLE TO EXTREME)

(WHISPER) Good morning darling. Time to get up. TAP! TAP!

HI JANIE! WOOF! GET UP YOU SLEEPY HEAD! ARF! ARF!

MOOO MOOOO IT'S TIME TO MOOOVE!

BEEP! BEEP! HEY YOU BONEHEADS! OUTTA THE SACK! TIME'S NOW 7:20! LET'S LOOK AT TRAFFIC! WHOA! BACK-UPS! PILE-UPS!

HUG AND KISS → ENTERTAINMENT → ALARM CLOCK → ALARM CLOCK RADIO →

morning listening to loud music and/or offensive radio "personalities."

DRESSING

Clothing that will be worn the next day should be chosen the night before. This avoids last-minute surprises, such as the possibility that a desired garment is in the wash or that more than one person plans to wear it. Also, it is easier to negotiate the wearing of temperature-appropriate clothing or stained and ripped items of dubious acceptability without the distraction of a honking schoolbus.

Some moms even go so far as to dress their children in tomorrow's clothing before putting

BLANKET REMOVAL

> GOOD NIGHT, DEAR.
>
> 'NITE, MOM.

them to bed, thereby insuring a real head start, but for many this is a bit *too* efficient.

GROOMING

See **How to Wash Up,** pp. 80–81.

BREAKFAST

The perfect breakfast would be a doughnut that is nutritionally identical to a glass of juice and a bowl of cereal, milk, and fresh fruit. Until that day comes, the juice, cereal, milk, and fruit is recommended. Putting any nonperishables on the table the night before is also a timesaver. Or offer a one-hand, eat-on-the-bus special:

- Boxed juice
- Cored apple with peanut butter in middle
- Rice cakes with apple butter or peanut butter
- String cheese and crackers
- Instant breakfast drink served in disposable container
- Bagel with cream cheese
- Nutritionally correct muffin (low fat, preferably with fiber)

TO SPEED DEPARTURE, SOME MOMS SET THE BREAKFAST TABLE THE NIGHT BEFORE...

BUT DO NOT PUT OUT CEREAL IF YOU HAVE PESTS...

> Any puffies left?
>
> I think I see the toy!

Puffed Puffies FREE TOY!

OR DUST.

SEPARATING

Your child will tell you when he or she feels old enough to walk to school without you. Arrange instead for the child to walk with friends. Repress the urge to come along anyway, disguised (so as not to embarrass your child) as Escorto the Clown.

If your child takes the bus and does not want to be accompanied to the pickup, peeking through the front door until you actually see the child board the bus is perfectly acceptable, though perhaps not to your child.

CHILDREN WHO THINK THEY ARE WALKING TO SCHOOL BY THEMSELVES.
(Can you find the moms hiding in this picture?)

How to Make Chocolate Treats

One surefire way to impress your child in the kitchen is to learn how to twirl dough like a pizza chef. Another is to produce any kind of treat made of chocolate.

There are at least three reasons why making chocolate treats is a more sensible choice. One, it is easier for children to help stir chocolate treats than to assist in twirling the pizza dough. Two, it is more fun to lick the mixing bowl than to lick the pizza pan. And three, when you make chocolate treats, you won't have to clean the ceiling (usually).

CHOCOLATE PUDDING

There is no such thing as bad chocolate pudding, but some are better than others. Packaged instant pudding—unlike *true* instant pudding, which is bought ready-to-eat—takes just slightly longer than an instant. You add milk to the mix, shake or stir it for a minute or two, and shortly thereafter it arrives at puddinghood. However, it never quite achieves the extremely desirable, sludgelike texture of cooked pudding. (It is okay to make cooked pudding from a mix. Making it from scratch is mom overachieving). Cooked pudding requires slow cooking and stirring over the flame and then an hour or two to set. As a reward for this lesson in patience, the cooking spoon can be licked and the pan can be scraped.

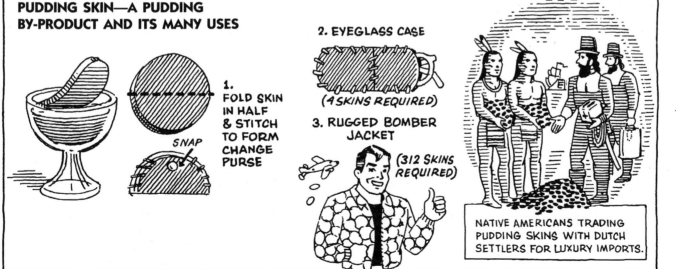

PUDDING SKIN—A PUDDING BY-PRODUCT AND ITS MANY USES

SNAP

1. FOLD SKIN IN HALF & STITCH TO FORM CHANGE PURSE

2. EYEGLASS CASE

(4 SKINS REQUIRED)

3. RUGGED BOMBER JACKET

(312 SKINS REQUIRED)

NATIVE AMERICANS TRADING PUDDING SKINS WITH DUTCH SETTLERS FOR LUXURY IMPORTS.

Ingredients

2 cups of milk
3.5 oz. package of pudding mix

1. Pour the dry mix into a saucepan and add two cups of milk.

2. Stirring continuously, bring the mixture to a boil.

3. Remove from heat. Pour into one large bowl or four small dishes. Mixture will thicken as it cools.

Note: It is hard to improve upon chocolate pudding, but some folks sprinkle nuts or chocolate chips on top of the pudding shortly before it is set and use a spoon to swirl them in. Whipped cream for the top isn't bad either.

HOT COCOA

Luncheonette owners, who brew cocoa from a mix, say that there are several schools of thought about cocoa, but the major division is between those who add it to milk and those who add it to water. It may be topped with whipped cream and/or marshmallows.

The height of chocolatey indulgence is cocoa made directly from chocolate.

Ingredients

12-oz. semisweet chocolate bar
3½ cups milk

1. Chop chocolate or shave it into strips with a vegetable peeler or put it into a food processor.

2. Scald milk. (Scalding means putting it on high heat but leaving it there only until, when you shake the pot, the milk makes a "Sssss" sound, like escaping steam.)

3. Turn off the heat and stir in the chocolate.

4. Bring the liquid to a simmer (small bubbles appear around the edges of the pot), stirring frequently. Serve in large cups, preferably on a very cold day in front of a fireplace.

CHOCOLATE CHIP COOKIES

Cookies made with classic recipes may still vary from home to home and even from batch to batch. Some cookies are flatter than others. Some will have more chips. And some may be golden brown all over while others are black on the bottom, especially if you get a telephone call in the middle and forget to take them out of the oven. All of them are delicious, though

the ones that are black on the bottom are
somewhat less so.

CHOCOLATE CHIP COOKIES

Ingredients

2¼ cups flour
1 teaspoon baking soda
¾ teaspoon salt
2 sticks (½ pound) unsalted butter, softened
¾ cup granulated sugar
¾ cup packed brown sugar
1¼ teaspoons vanilla extract
2 eggs
1 package (12 ounces) semisweet or
    bittersweet chocolate chips

1. Preheat oven to 375°F. In a medium bowl,
combine flour, baking soda, and salt. Stir or whisk
gently to mix.

2. In a large bowl, beat butter until soft and light.
Gradually mix in granulated sugar and brown
sugar; beat until smooth and fluffy. Add eggs one
at a time, mixing well after each addition. Beat in
vanilla.

3. Gradually add flour mixture, mixing until well
blended. Stir in chocolate chips.

4. Drop cookie dough by heaping teaspoons 2
inches apart onto ungreased baking sheets. Bake
10 minutes, or until cookies are lightly browned
around the edges. Transfer to a wire rack and let
cool completely. Store in an airtight container.

Makes 60 to 70 cookies.

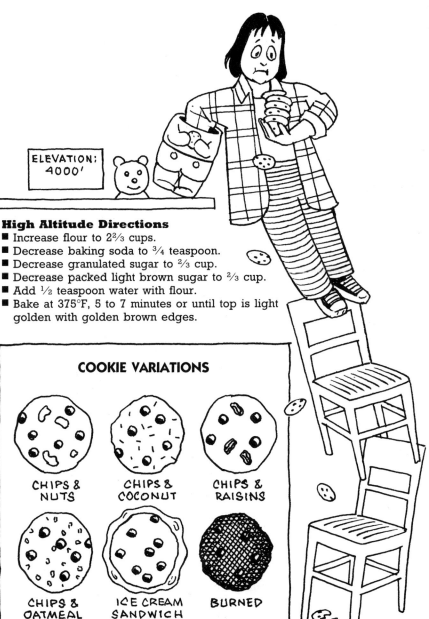

ELEVATION:
4000'

High Altitude Directions
- Increase flour to 2⅔ cups.
- Decrease baking soda to ¾ teaspoon.
- Decrease granulated sugar to ⅔ cup.
- Decrease packed light brown sugar to ⅔ cup.
- Add ½ teaspoon water with flour.
- Bake at 375°F, 5 to 7 minutes or until top is light
  golden with golden brown edges.

COOKIE VARIATIONS

CHIPS &
NUTS

CHIPS &
COCONUT

CHIPS &
RAISINS

CHIPS &
OATMEAL

ICE CREAM
SANDWICH

BURNED

How to Care for a Pet

The only thing possibly cuter than the sight of your child is the sight of your child snuggling with a pet. Not only may a pet be your child's most reliable best friend but also owning a pet teaches empathy and compassion and—say the experts—what is required to care for another living thing. The notion seems to be that having pets when you are little makes you more likely to remember to feed, groom, and walk your human children when you are grown up. Even if this is not so, every kid enjoys having a pet and sometimes so does mom.

animal that may set off anyone's allergies or requires more maintenance than you can handle. Think carefully about personality types: you may realize that certain breeds of dogs aren't suitable around children, but it's less obvious that an excitable bird is not a good match for a high-spirited young child.

The ideal first pet, of course, is a clam. You can pick it up and put it down and pick it up and put it down and pick it up and put it down and pick it up and put it down and it won't object. If it's dropped, nothing happens. And

WHO CARES FOR THE PET? – THE RESPONSIBILITY SHIFT

■ = % OF PET CHILD FEELS RESPONSIBLE FOR
□ = % OF PET PARENT IS RESPONSIBLE FOR

| UPON PURCHASE | AFTER FIRST WALK | AFTER PET BARKS ALL NIGHT |

Consult with a vet, breeder, and/or reputable pet store manager before shopping for a pet. Otherwise, you may go home with a beguiling puppy who grows to the size of a sofa or an attractive parrot who develops an attitude problem. Don't even consider any

then you can cook it for supper. Of course, your child probably had something furry in mind.

No matter what the final choice, you will be faced with one pet-owning hurdle or another. Consider the following examples.

HOW TO BATHE A DOG

Dogs did not evolve to be bathed in tiled bathrooms. As a rule of thumb, dog baths are best given outdoors; the larger the dog, the more this holds true. And remember that although dogs like to splash, they do not enjoy being the splashee. If you are using a hose-type attachment, keep it close to the dog's body.

Beverly Hills, the dog-washing expert who founded Laundermutt, advises the following procedure:

1. Use tepid water and pet shampoo. (Exception: if your dog needs a dandruff shampoo, get the kind humans use.)

2. Put cotton balls in the ears and a drop of baby oil in each eye.

3. Wet down dog with hose-type attachment or bucket of water or sponge.

4. Apply shampoo with sponge and massage gently into every nook and cranny.

5. Rinse head. Use a sponge and don't get soap or water in dog's eyes, ears, or nostrils. Then rinse body with sponge, hose, or bucket. Make sure all soap is out.

6. Use one fluffy towel to squeeze water out gently and a second to rub your pet briskly.

DOG WASHING DIRECTIONS:

- Tail to nose when lathering
- Nose to tail when rinsing
- Top to bottom

WASH CYCLE   **RINSE CYCLE**

HOW TO CATCH A HAMSTER

Once a hamster, gerbil, or mouse has been welcomed (as opposed to having burrowed) into your home, it will look for any opportunity to leave its cage to explore other parts. Small rodents are tremendously flexible. A mouse, for example, can squeeze its way into an opening the size of a nickel and won't pass up the challenge.

Impress on your child the need to remember this important rule: Always put the top back on the cage. But when, inevitably, the rule is broken, reassure your child that the escaped hamster (mouse, gerbil) can be retrieved.

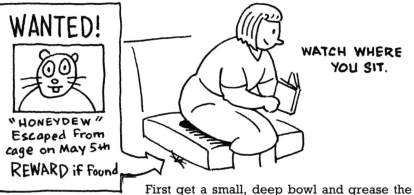

WANTED!

"HONEYDEW"
Escaped from
cage on May 5th
REWARD if found

WATCH WHERE
YOU SIT.

First get a small, deep bowl and grease the sides with oil. In the middle, put a bit of the hamster's favorite food or a little bit of peanut butter. Then position a book as a ramp that leads to the edge of the bowl. During the next night or two, chances are excellent that the hungry pet will sniff out the food, climb up the ramp, and land in the middle of the bowl. There it will remain until someone comes to the rescue.

HOW TO CONDUCT A PET FUNERAL

As long as goldfish continue to be awarded as carnival prizes, young children will experience one of the harsh realities of the life cycle for the first time when, overfed or unused to living in a bowl unequipped with elaborate filtration systems, the fish succumb.

To prepare your child for such a loss, it is helpful to suggest that certain types of animals have a very short life expectancy and that goldfish—which you may prefer to call "dayfish"—are among them.

There is something positive to be learned from the death of a small pet. It is a rite of passage that may prompt your child's first questions about human life and death and lead the child to explore not just his or her own

feelings but also yours. If mom treats the loss solemnly, your child will feel not only comforted but respected. But take your cue from your child in handling the situation. A child who is willing to flush the pet away should not be coerced into holding a funeral.

If a funeral *is* desired, you'll need a small box, lined with a bit of cotton or soft cloth, in which to bury the pet. (Note: Do-it-yourself funerals are recommended only for animals smaller than a soap dish.) If you have no backyard, interment may take place in a large potted plant. Or you may prefer to choose a place at some distance from home so no one is tempted to disturb the remains.

The service may include a hymn, a prayer, and/or a eulogy. Use a laundry marking pen on a tongue depresser or popsickle stick as a grave marker and place or plant a flower at the spot.

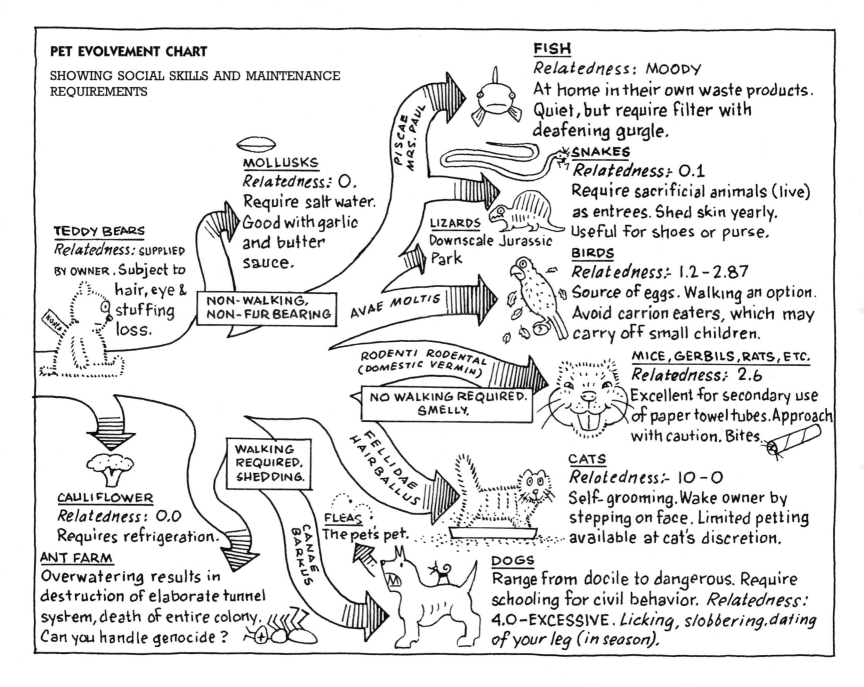

PET EVOLVEMENT CHART

SHOWING SOCIAL SKILLS AND MAINTENANCE REQUIREMENTS

FISH
Relatedness: MOODY
At home in their own waste products. Quiet, but require filter with deafening gurgle.

PISCAE MRS. PAUL

MOLLUSKS
Relatedness: 0.
Require salt water. Good with garlic and butter sauce.

SNAKES
Relatedness: 0.1
Require sacrificial animals (live) as entrees. Shed skin yearly. Useful for shoes or purse.

LIZARDS
Downscale Jurassic Park

TEDDY BEARS
Relatedness: SUPPLIED BY OWNER. Subject to hair, eye & stuffing loss.

NON-WALKING, NON-FUR BEARING

AVAE MOLTIS

BIRDS
Relatedness: 1.2 - 2.87
Source of eggs. Walking an option. Avoid carrion eaters, which may carry off small children.

RODENTI RODENTAL (DOMESTIC VERMIN)

NO WALKING REQUIRED. SMELLY.

MICE, GERBILS, RATS, ETC.
Relatedness: 2.6
Excellent for secondary use of paper towel tubes. Approach with caution. Bites.

WALKING REQUIRED, SHEDDING.

FELLIDAE HAIRBALLUS

CAULIFLOWER
Relatedness: 0.0
Requires refrigeration.

CANAE BARKUS

FLEAS
The pet's pet.

CATS
Relatedness: 10 - 0
Self-grooming. Wake owner by stepping on face. Limited petting available at cat's discretion.

ANT FARM
Overwatering results in destruction of elaborate tunnel system, death of entire colony. Can you handle genocide?

DOGS
Range from docile to dangerous. Require schooling for civil behavior. *Relatedness:* 4.0 - EXCESSIVE. *Licking, slobbering, dating of your leg (in season).*

How to Make a Halloween Costume

TAKE FROM THE RICH...

PRANK OR PLUNDER

Unfortunately, creating even the most artistic and original Halloween costume may not win you any points from a child who prefers to be one of the pack.

No matter how many hours you spend bleaching a pajama sleeper and attaching yarn hair to make it indistinguishable from an actual Palomino pony, and no matter how much loving care and yardage you put into producing a clown costume that looks just like the one on the pattern package, your child may prefer to come dressed in a tacky plastic outfit as the superhero *du jour*.

Before you begin work on a Halloween costume, investigate your child's wishes. If the tacky plastic outfit is what the child wants, buy it and save your creative skills for future mom-child projects like making a three-dimensional map of Brazil or constructing a shoebox diorama of Grecian daily life.

If the child does want your Halloween suggestions, here are some easy (and last-minute) solutions:

Robin Hood: Make a tunic from a green garbage bag with slits cut for head and arms. Add belt and tights. Staple leaves to the bag to keep Robin camouflaged in Sherwood Forest. As a matter of fact, a companion may go along in a second, beltless, completely leaf-covered garbage bag—as Sherwood Forest.

Ghost: Cut eyeholes in a sheet.

TRICKIUM OR TREATIUS

Ancient Roman: Drape a sheet over one shoulder; belt with rope. Add sandals and a crown of leaves.

OTHER QUICK COSTUMES

Leotards and tights in various colors suggest a whole range of possibilities:

■ To black tights, add collar and cuffs, bow tie, tail, and ears. Paint on whiskers and you've got a kitten.

■ To red tights, add a crown and cape. Staple on playing cards and say hello to the Queen (King) of Hearts (Diamonds)!

■ To pink tights, add a large diaper (made from a pillowcase), an oversize pacifier, a baby bottle, and a blankie and there's a big baby.

■ To green tights, add a crown with petals and you've got a flower. A group of little girls could come together as a bouquet. For another group effort, several children, each dressed in a single bright color, can go together as a rainbow.

■ Trunks, a towel, a cape, and a "black eye" make a boxer.

■ A tie-dyed shirt plus love beads, a headband, peace symbols, and round glasses make a hippie.

■ Or cut arm and leg holes in a large cardboard box, decorate it with gift wrap and ribbons, and put a bow in your child's hair: she's a present. Or paint it white and add dots, and your little one is half of a pair of dice.

EARS

Tape paper cut-out ears to headband

43

How to Give a Bath

It is one of the essential paradoxes of childhood that it is hard to persuade the child to get into the tub at bathtime and then it is impossible to get the child out of it.

Though you will supervise the lathering and rinsing of younger children, when they reach age five or so, they may feel capable of bathing themselves. However, many children "take a bath" just as they "wash their hands"—without soap. The best way to confirm this is to touch the bar of soap. If it is dry, it probably has not been used.

The childhood trauma most routinely inflicted on children is shampoo in the eyes. Remedies run the gamut from the ineffective (vaseline on the forehead) to the elaborate (ski masks). But there are two easy and workable solutions: slip a small plastic inner tube over your child's head and have your child lean back against it; or have your child look straight up at the ceiling and cup your hand under the child's head.

TUB ACTIVITIES THAT SHOULD BE DISCOURAGED

DRINKING THE BATHWATER

SWIMMING UNDERWATER

DIVING RINGS

SHAMPOOING PROVIDES HAIRSTYLING OPPORTUNITIES

"SPIKE" "TROLL" "DAIRY QUEEN"

MOM HOLDS MIRROR

MAKING
TIDAL
WAVES

PULLING
THE PLUG

The popularity of the rubber duck has of course been celebrated in story and song. But all water toys add greatly to the entertainment value of the bath. Very young children may be entertained with any containers that can be used for pouring, though older ones will progress to more and more complicated items. However, the total volume of the bath toys should at no point exceed the total volume of the bath water.

How to Start a Business

Your child may have dreams—acquisitive, big-ticket, American dreams, dreams that cannot be realized with the measly allowance you dole out. Sooner or later, The Spirit That Made This Country Great will awaken in your child, who will then ask, "How can I make more money?"

There are those who are willing to pay for the execution of household chores. But there are many others who are high-minded about not putting a dollar value on tasks that should be done "simply because you are part of the family." (These folks have also considered the danger of introducing labor unrest into the family union.)

Besides, as a general principle, *dues unto others.* In other words, it is always preferable to tap sources outside the family for extra cash. Encourage your child's entreprenurial initiative by proposing any of the following.

THE LEMONADE STAND
The prime spot for this low-risk money maker is on a route with heavy jogger traffic. From a one-item operation, children may expand the menu with cookies, iced tea, and—of course—"sports" drinks. (Note: It's your call whether this will be an untarnished experience in the joy of making money or a lesson in reality. If the latter, deduct the cost of the raw materials.)

THE FLEA MARKET OR YARD SALE
A child's chance to be divested of unwanted toys.

THE CAR WASH
A less passive and wetter entrepreneurial activity than a stand, the car wash offers children the opportunity to earn money by spraying one another with a hose. As in the shower, where you wash your hair first, work from the top—in this case, the roof—down. A portable vacuum adds a cleaning "extra."

THE FARM STAND

As any retailer knows, the key to success is location, location, location, and nowhere is this more true than in the case of a farm stand. A child who sets up zucchini on a deserted road or on I-80 is destined for a disappointing day in the sun. Drivers seldom brake for a child with a zucchini. Warning signs are, therefore, a prerequisite for successful roadside sales.

The choicest location for a child's stand is not on a road at all, but outside the supermarket—unless, of course, the market owner can't stand the competition.

SELF-SERVICE GREENMARKET

A modern marketing concept born of boredom and low-volume traffic.

PET SITTING

If your child likes to take care of animals, advertise his or her availability to walk dogs, change the hamster's chips, or open a can for kitty while owners are away.

For the younger child who likes to pour water, Plant Care is a less challenging vocational choice.

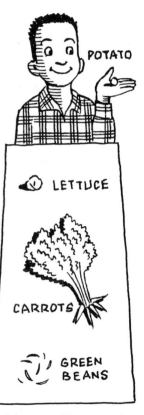

A farm stand is a natural outlet for the bounty of a child's garden. Unfortunately, in their rush to riches, children will not wait for things to ripen, so their produce will be small and greenish.

H--w t-- Pack a Suitcase

A CHILD PACKS:

A MOTHER PACKS:

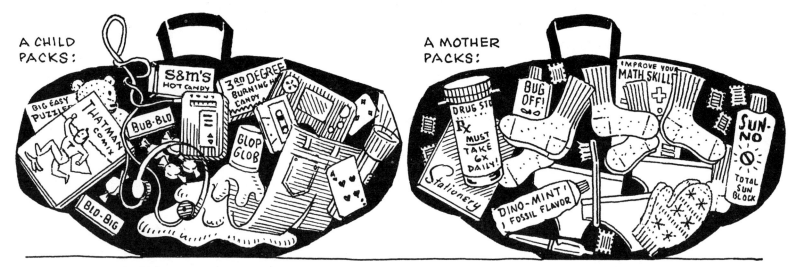

Children pack only what they believe they need, a list that remains pretty much the same no matter where they are going or what weather conditions may prevail. Generally, they will remember to include all their essential games, toys, Walkmans, and sports equipment. They may also take along one or more favorite T-shirts, possibly some jeans, and maybe an extra pair of sneakers. But it is definitely up to mom to remember dress clothing, socks, underwear, pajamas, medicine, toothbrush, and/or other toiletry items, including the dental retainer.

The simplest way to make sure your child brings everything that is necessary is to provide a checklist. For a child who is too young to read but eager to help (an attitude that should be encouraged), draw a simple picture of *each* item that should be packed. For

a five-day trip, you might draw five sets of underwear and socks but only one pair of pajamas, for example.

If dressy clothes are not involved, it may be most efficient to pack an entire day's outfit in a large zipper-lock plastic bag. At the end of the

day, everything goes back into the bag and from there directly into the laundry.

Of course, there is only one way to make absolutely sure children have everything they need with them and that is to have them stay home.

A SPECIAL NOTE ON PACKING FOR CAMP

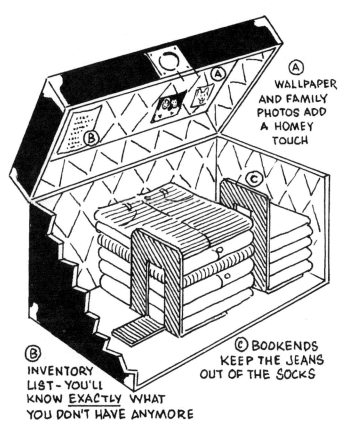

(A) WALLPAPER AND FAMILY PHOTOS ADD A HOMEY TOUCH

(C) BOOKENDS KEEP THE JEANS OUT OF THE SOCKS

(B) INVENTORY LIST- YOU'LL KNOW <u>EXACTLY</u> WHAT YOU DON'T HAVE ANYMORE

Many of the items that are sent to camp never come out of the trunk. The bright side of having your child come home with underwear and socks still in the package is that you will have less to shop for in the fall—provided, of course, that the items still fit.

Experienced moms send a child to camp with only the shabbiest underwear (if it gets lost, you'll be relieved) and the ugliest, brightest towels. (The more distinctive the gear, the more likely it is to get back from the laundry to the right camper.)

Before the season begins, the camp will undoubtedly provide you with a list of "necessities." The list will include some

WHY DID MOM PACK A MONOGRAMMED ROBE AND SLIPPERS?

I HAVEN'T USED THIS NINE IRON ALL SUMMER.

difficult-to-locate items whose utility you may question but which you will be certain to send along. These, too, will probably come home in the original packaging, for your child will not know what to make of them either.

No matter what you send, your child will request additional garments throughout the summer, depending on what "cool" things other children have. You may find you look forward to these requests since otherwise you might get no mail from camp at all.

Most things that return from camp aren't worth the shipping costs.

How to Take a Car Trip That Doesn't Drive You Crazy

The image of the family rolling across the miles while singing "You Are My Sunshine" in multipart harmony may be an appealing one but it tends to happen mostly in movies that are promoted as "family entertainment." In real life, if everyone is still on speaking terms at the end of the trip, it qualifies as a success.

REFRESHMENTS

Car travel is very dehydrating to children. In fact, most begin asking for a drink the moment they are strapped into the car seat and many will ask for food besides. You can save a lot of

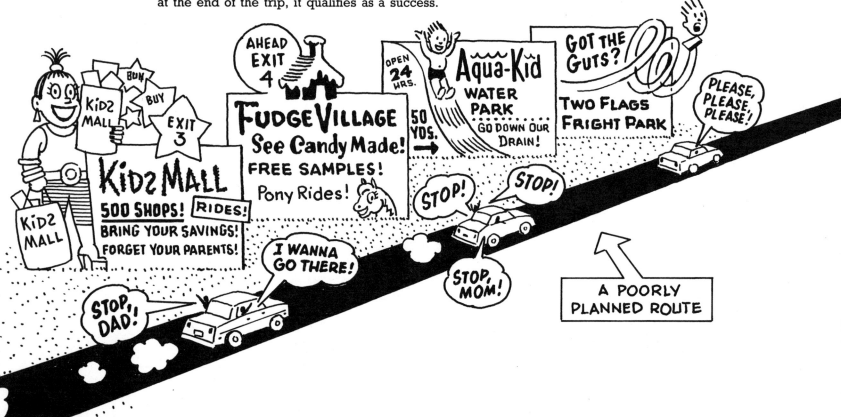

money (and time) by bringing drinks and snacks from home, even counting the cost of cleaning the upholstery.

(Note: A child who is susceptible to motion sickness should not be encouraged to eat much before or during the ride, or to read in the car. To avoid or quell motion sickness, tell the child to look at a distant spot out the car window. But carry a bucket with disposable liner anyway.)

Eating and drinking inevitably leads to rest stops. Children have radar systems for bathrooms that, interestingly, work in reverse. Passing the exit ramp of a service area sends the signal "Empty me now" directly to the child's bladder, particularly if the next service area is at least 25 miles away. If you do not consider it a grand adventure to leave the freeway and roam back roads in search of a toilet, stop at all service areas and insist the child visit the bathroom irrespective of the child's assessment of the need to go.

"ARE WE THERE YET?"

Warning your child in advance that you do not plan to make unscheduled stops at petting zoos, miniature golf ranges, flea circuses, military museums, or the like will simply whet the child's appetite for these attractions. Avoid such statements, and try to travel on routes that have strict ordinances regarding billboards. However, though this will permit you to get where you're going faster, it will also accelerate the boredom and complaint level.

Other side effects of long car trips are periodic scuffling and uncontrollable laughter. Seating a grandparent or other large object between the children is one means of

prevention, but if this is impractical, buy earplugs. Even better, try to get some group activity going.

Music is helpful. Sing together or bring in

the pros—on tape. But unless everyone shares the same enthusiasm for 24 consecutive replays of, say, Barney the Dinosaur, provide individual cassette players and headsets.

Or try some traditional car games:

Alphabet Sentences. Make up an entire sentence—as long as you can—of words beginning only with A (though you may also use little words such as "a," "the," "to," "at," "in," and other prepositions and conjunctions); next player makes a sentence of B words. The player who has used the most words wins. For example: Alden asks Allison about amusing animals at the aquarium.

Billboard Alphabet. Player looks for an "a" in the first road sign that is passed.

Whether or not player succeeds, next player takes a turn. Continue until all players have found A. Then players each take a turn looking for "B," and so on. This may be played cooperatively, or one player may take signs on the left and the other takes signs on the right; hard-to-find letters (q, x, z) may be ruled out.

Ghost. First player names any letter of the alphabet and next player adds a letter. The idea is to spell a word—but not to have the word end at your turn. (Words must be longer than three letters.) If the word ends with you, you get a "G." First player to get "G-H-O-S-T" is out.

First Player: B
Second Player: U
Third Player: S
Fourth Player: If player says T, round ends. If player says I (thinking of the word "business"), game passes to Fifth Player, and so on.

Grandmother's Trunk. First player says, "In grandmother's trunk I found an [name an item beginning with A]." Next player repeats sentence, adding ". . . and a [item beginning with B]." Continue in this fashion. Players who can't come up with an item or who can't remember the *whole* list are out.

Geography. Player mentions any place name. The next player must choose a place name that begins with the last letter of that name. For example: Arkansas/**S**an Francisc**o**/**O**rego**n**/**N**ew York.

How to Draw a Family Tree

In addition to producing new twigs, moms generally chart the growth of the family tree. Moms always seem to know how you and cousin Leonard are related (your great-grandmothers were sisters) and why your children won't inherit great-uncle Marvin's famous ears (because he isn't a blood relative; he just married into the family).

There are several reasons to draw a family tree:

1. It is nice to have the drawing for posterity.

2. A drawing may make it easier to understand family relationships, in comparison to which trigonometry seems simple.

3. When your child gets around to asking, "Where did I come from?" drawing a family tree is an easy alternative to explaining Darwinian evolution or introducing the business about the birds and the bees.

A SIMPLE FAMILY TREE

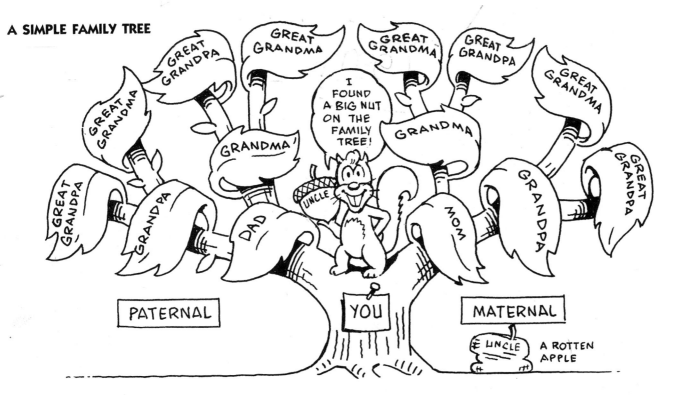

How to do the Laundry

Once someone invented a machine to wash clothes, it was merely a matter of time until the task was no longer gender-specific. Unlike dishwashing, which involves sharp objects, sorting, loading, and folding are generally safe and foolproof activities that will engage your child.

Unfortunately, by the time they are old enough to handle advanced concepts such as "temperature settings" and "bleach" or "detergent," children are more interested in talking on the phone than in doing laundry. Their interest in the latter will remain dormant until they are about to leave for college and become responsible for cleaning their own clothes.

SORTING

Having mastered the subtleties of sorting, you yourself may occasionally decide to throw caution to the wind and mix something red with something white, but your child, a beginning sorter, should be given very rigid guidelines:

1. Do not wash fuzzy items (like sweatshirts and towels) with items that attract fuzz, like corduroy and shiny, synthetic fabrics, or your Lycra tights will look as if they're growing hair.

2. Do not mix colored items with white items.

MAP SHOWING MIGRATORY PATHS OF LINT

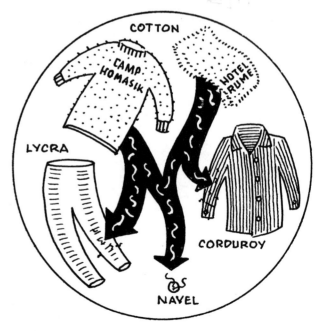

54

LOADING

1. Check all pockets before putting anything into the machine. Remove coins or small toys (which can jam the works), crayons (which can stain), and wads of tissues (which will dissolve into small and very tenacious tufts of paper).

2. Zip zippers. Button buttons. Hook hooks.

3. Do not cram the wash into the machine. When laundry is agitated—just like humans who are agitated—it needs space.

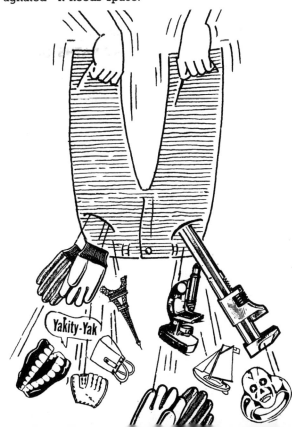

Yakity-Yak

HOW TO BATHE A BEAR

1. PUT TEDDY INTO A PILLOW CASE

2. CLOSE WITH A RUBBER BAND AND WASH

3. DRY WITH A HAIR DRYER AS YOU BRUSH OR HANG UP

4. DO NOT PUT TEDDY INTO A DRYER, OR YOU'LL GET... BALDIE BEAR!

FOLDING

One reason folding is such a nice activity is that freshly dried laundry smells almost as good as popcorn. Also, folding introduces your child to the concepts of neatness and organization and to one of the great mysteries of life—where do odd socks go?

The most important rule in the laundry room: Never turn on the machine without first checking where the pet is.

H--w t-- Find T--i--

Scientists say human eyes are so sensitive that on a clear night when there is no moon, a person sitting on a mountain peak can see a match struck 30 miles away. If that is so, why is mom the only one who can locate the cream cheese at the back of the refrigerator or the sneakers at the bottom of the closet?

One explanation is that moms are the ones who assign places to most of the items in the house. So naturally, moms are the persons most likely to notice when a wrong thing is in the right place and vice versa.

Furthermore, patience and perseverance are inherent to the role of mom, developed in the course of waiting for an egg to hatch or baby to emerge. The others in the family have to be taught these skills.

FINDING AN ITEM THAT IS NOT NECESSARILY LOST BUT MERELY HIDDEN FROM VIEW

You may find it useful to post the following list of places where the item may be. Tell your child to go through it before calling you in:

- The rear of the refrigerator shelf
- The door of the refrigerator
- Under the bed
- Under the sofa
- In the junk drawer
- Between the sofa pillows
- Between the bed and the wall
- In the dirty clothes hamper
- In the dryer
- On the floor of the closet
- In another family member's closet
- On the top shelf of the closet
- In a coat pocket
- Under the front seat of the car
- On the floor of the car
- In the trunk of the car
- On the desk
- In the place where it's supposed to be

FINDING AN ITEM THAT IS ACTUALLY LOST

A child who has lost something will generally go through these four stages:

1. Denial: *It's not lost. It's just been put someplace and I can't remember where.* Refer to list above. If that is fruitless, the child will proceed to step 2.

2. Anger: *Someone else moved it.* Once denials have been issued, child will move on to step 3.

3. Grief: *What will I do without it?* Having worked this through, child will continue to step 4.

4. Acceptance: *Everything is somewhere. It may be lost, but it must be somewhere.*

Mom can aid a child who has reached the stage of acceptance in one or more of the following ways.

Whimsical approach: Role playing. Ask: If you were [the lost item], where would you be?

Learning opportunity: Aided recall. Ask: Where did you use it last? Did you bring it home from school? From your sleepover? Did you lend it to anyone?

Immersion in reality: Pressure's on. Say: You've got to find that one because I will not buy you another.

How to Give a Birthday Party

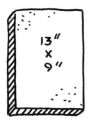

Kings and queens may have their inaugurations and brides and grooms their wedding day, but these milestones are probably no more eagerly anticipated than a child's birthday. Even very young children look forward to this special day as a marker of growth (which usually means additional privileges and importance) and an opportunity to be the center of attention. The presents are pretty nice, too.

Children enjoy planning the party almost as much as experiencing it—in fact, because they are often so keyed up on the big day, sometimes even more! Keep plans manageable enough so that you can pay most of your attention to the birthday child. What matters far more than details is simply whether your child has a good time. And remember, you've got a whole year to get ready for the next one.

GUEST LIST

The child/adult ratio is more important than the size of the guest list. There should be at least one adult per child until the age of four. After that, factor in such variables as the maturity of the child, the availability of older sibling helpers, the size of the room, and, perhaps,

whether or not the parent(s) is (are) taking Prozac™.

LETTING SOMEONE ELSE DO IT

Most fast-food operations run children's parties on their premises. Advertised in the local newspaper, you will also find hair salons that run hair-styling parties for little girls, gyms that offer gym parties, craft shops that supervise craft-making parties, and so on. Many such facilities provide refreshments, cake, and even favors. Bonus: Limit on length of party; few surprises; no cleanup. Drawback: Cost; also, may lack personal touch.

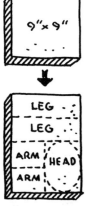

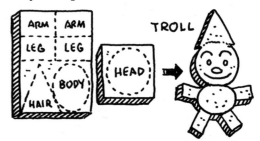

MISS MOOSE MAY BE A TURKEY

DOING IT YOURSELF (MODIFIED)

Even if you have a party at home, you may decide to hire entertainment to get you through the difficult moments (which is pretty much the entire interval between the guests' arrival and the serving of the cake). Always preview the act. And bear in mind that no matter how magical the magician or comical the clown, some children will be enthralled, others will be frightened and/or bored. (That, as they say, is show business.) Acts involving animals are generally welcomed enthusiastically

WHEELS

BODY

BODY

WINDOWS

STRETCH LIMO

by everyone except the mom in whose home the party is being held.

DOING IT YOURSELF (TRADITIONAL)

If you have enough room and an adventurous spirit, in lieu of packaged entertainment you may want to play the traditional party games. Because they have now become a novelty, these are often surprisingly enjoyable. Older siblings and extra parents should be recruited as referees, judges, and the like. Games may include:

■ Bean bag: A bean bag must be thrown into some kind of a goal, such as a wastepaper basket.

■ Three-legged race: Pairs of children race other pairs; their two inside legs are tied together.

■ Pin the Tail on the Donkey, Pin the Nose on the Witch, and so on: A blindfolded child attempts to place the missing part correctly.

■ Potato race: A relay race in which teams carry a potato on a spoon from one place to another.

■ Musical chairs: Children march around a line of chairs set up so that seats face in alternate directions, with one chair fewer than the number of children. When the music stops, children must sit; the child without a seat and one more chair are both eliminated.

VENUS

WE ALSO OFFER TOURNEDOS ROSSINI AND ENDIVES BRAISÉES.

■ Limbo: Children must sidle underneath a pole (held by two people or propped across the backs of two chairs) without touching hands to the ground; pole is lowered each time all the children have gone through or been eliminated.

DOING IT YOURSELF (TRADITIONAL WITH THEME)

Teddy Bear Party In this nice variation that may please very young boys and girls, each guest is invited to come along with a favorite stuffed bear. Instead of musical chairs, play Musical Bears (the teddies are carried around a table and are "seated" on place mats) and pin the honey jar on the bear's palm, and have guests limbo under a "bear tree" branch. Give each guest a small cardboard teddy to "decorate" with craft items such as bows, buttons, ribbons, and the like that can be glued on with the help of an older child or adult; these go home as the party favors. Gummi bears are served and the cake, of course, is in the shape of a bear.

FOOD AND DRINK

If you are serving at home, there is no reason you should feel obliged to include a meal in the party plans, but if you do, here are the possibilities: pizza. Do not even think about anything else. Pizza is the universal kids' food, though there is occasionally a contrary guest who will request something unexpected, such as chicken fingers. Since you may not have these on hand, it is reasonable to offer a cheese sandwich or a peanut butter and jelly sandwich instead. The children will drink juice, but only if there is no soda.

The main event is the cake. Ice cream cakes are popular, but it's always a bit dicey dealing with food that is likely to change states if there is a delay in serving it. Anyway, children are less interested in the cake than the decorations. Since everyone wants a piece with a rose on it, you will be a hero if you offer a cake bedecked with at least one rose per person. For a similar reason, avoid the temptation to decorate the cake with cute little toys destined only for the birthday celebrant, since the guests will resent the fact that there are none for them and may even cry.

PRESENTS

Children under age four don't understand why the birthday child has all the presents and they get none, so it is wise to postpone the opening of the presents until after the guests have left. By the time they are six or seven the children may still feel jealous but have learned to put a lid on it.

THE PARTY BAGS

For the guests, anticipation regarding the party bags (also known as "treats" or "favors") is second only to the anticipation of the birthday cake itself. Quantity is probably more important than quality, though you may buy one single, interesting item. However, it is essential that no treat bag contain anything more than or different in the slightest way from any other bag. In any event, do not hand out the bags until the child is at the door wearing hat and coat and transportation has arrived. The bag eases the pain of departure and also, should one guest discover a minute variation in his/her treat bag or break one of the enclosed items immediately, it will not be your problem.

SLEEPOVERS

Older children graduate from the planned party to the sleepover. Guests provide their own sleeping bags and you provide the rented movies and/or video games and the eats: pizza, followed by popcorn, soda, and candy (by this age, interest in birthday cake has diminished). If you have been saying to yourself, "Gee, I'd love to observe the night sky—all night long" or would like to watch all 12 hours of Fassbinder's acclaimed film classic *Berlin Alexanderplatz* straight through, this is your chance. No one will get much sleep and at least one of the following is guaranteed to happen: there will be a pillow/food fight, the TV will break, someone will feel nauseated, someone will be ostracized, someone will cry, and everyone will be ready for breakfast at 6:00 A.M.

SQUALID CONDITIONS OF TYPICAL SLEEPOVER

61

How to Grow a Windowsill Farm

One of the all-time great moms, of course, is Mother Nature, who goes about her business without pause. At this moment, she is working her quiet miracles everywhere, perhaps even in the cheese drawer of your refrigerator where the mold is spreading on the Muenster. You may prefer a more controlled opportunity to help your child witness the miracle of plant growth.

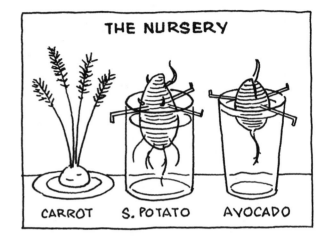

THE NURSERY

CARROT   S. POTATO   AVOCADO

"WHAT'S COMING UP, DOC?"

Help your little sprouts raise some sprouts of their own. Cut 1 inch off the top of a carrot and place the carrot top in a saucer of water. Put it on a sunny windowsill and within a few days shoots will appear. (Replace water as it is used up). The shoots will soon become delicate green leaves before your child's awestruck—or (worst case) indifferent—eyes.

NO CULTURE LIKE ACQUACULTURE

An avocado pit or sweet potato can provide a spectacular sort of growth experience. The avocado is better in a bright sun situation. Sweet potatoes prefer some shade. Suspend either in a jar of water, using skewers not currently being used to hold the stuffing in the turkey.

Obtaining the avocado pit may require the

preparation of guacamole (see following recipe). The ideal pit has cracked skin, belying a burgeoning stem trying to reach for the sky. Solid pits may grow nothing but mold.

Either the sweet potato vine or the avocado tree may be successfully transferred to soil and hence become full-fledged members of your houseplant family until blight doth you part.

GUACAMOLE
Ingredients

1 pitted avocado
¼ cup chopped onion
½ seeded, peeled tomato
1 tablespoon oil
¼ teaspoon chili powder
salt
pepper
mayonnaise

1. Mash flesh of avocado.

2. Stir in other ingredients.

3. Serve immediately with chips or refrigerate for later eating. (A thin layer of mayonnaise spread over the top prevents browning and can simply be stirred into the guacamole before it is served.)

HOW GREEN IS YOUR ALFALFA

Though growing a Chia pet may seem senseless, perhaps your child will enjoy growing a hairlike crop that is edible. A child who would turn up his nose at greens from the market might be persuaded to eat sprouts he has raised himself. Besides, this crop provides near-instant gratification: it sprouts in three to four days.

Put two tablespoons of alfalfa seed (from the natural foods store) into a straight-sided jar. (An empty 16-ounce peanut butter jar is ideal.)

Pour in cold water to a depth of about 2 inches. Let stand overnight.

In the morning, cover the opening with cheesecloth held in place by a rubber band, and drain off the water. Rinse the seeds with fresh water. Drain again.

Place the jar in a plastic bag, with the opening of the bag facing away from the jar top. Put the bagged jar in a cereal bowl, at an angle. The bag helps retain moisture. The angle helps the jar drain.

Rinse and drain again in the evening and thereafter in both the morning and at night. Continue until the first pair of leaves is almost ¼ inch tall. Then harvest.

NATURE'S BOUNTY

How to Set the Table

First came hunting, then came fire. Then, eventually, came tables, tablecloths, table manners, and other hallmarks of "civilization"—a subject of interest primarily to anthropologists and moms. Your child will probably wonder if keeping elbows off the table or using the right fork really matters. Moms know that if the child is elected president or wants to impress a date, someday it might.

Here's an easy way to help your child remember what goes where in a basic table setting.

■ "Fork" and "left" both have four letters. The fork goes on the left, and the napkin goes under it.

■ "Knife," "spoon," and "right" all have five letters. The knife and spoon go on the right.

The blade faces into the plate, so you don't cut yourself on it.

If there are extra forks or spoons in the place setting (a small salad fork, for example, or a large soup spoon) the general rule is that the one farthest from the plates are the ones that should be used first. Tell your child if he or she isn't sure what to do, watch the host and hostess and do as they do.

At the end of the meal, the fork and knife are put on an angle at the top right-hand side of the plate. The blade faces in.

Like the other parts of the table setting, the napkin has a purpose. It should be unfolded and put on your lap at the beginning of the meal and be kept out of sight unless it is lifted to wipe your mouth.

TABLE MANNERS

Right-handed Americans hold their fork in the right hand, transfer it to the left one for cutting, and then return it to the right hand for eating. Europeans keep their forks in the left hand for both cutting and eating. (Left-handed people do the reverse.) This means that on a transatlantic crossing, you will be correct no matter which hand you use.

Right: Holding your fork like a pen, so it rests lightly between the second and third fingers and is held in place by the thumb

Wrong: Holding your fork like a spear

It is polite to wait until everyone at the table has been served before starting to eat, no matter how long the table is.

Chewing, which is done with the mouth closed, should never be confused with talking, which is done with the mouth open. Attempts to do both at once should be discouraged. Though easier than patting your stomach and rubbing your head at the same time, it offends table companions.

Explain that if there is a dish the child does not wish to eat, it is sufficient to say, "No thank you." It is unnecessary to say, "Yuck," clutch your throat, stick out your tongue, bug out your eyes, and/or make gagging noises.

Encourage subjects that are appropriate for table talk (What I Learned at School Today, Why I'm Looking Forward to Grandmother's Visit, My Goals for the Future, and other high-minded topics) and discourage subjects that are provocative (How Come I Always Get Blamed for Everything, Why Can't I Have a Pet Snake) or distasteful (What Happened in the School Lunchroom, Interesting Wounds Sustained by Classmates).

When leaving the table during the meal, it is polite to say, "May I be excused?" but unnecessary to add that you are going to the bathroom. You also say, "May I be excused?" when you have finished eating. It is considerate not to leave the table until the others have finished eating, though this is often beyond the endurance of many children, particularly if coffee is being served. It is not unreasonable, however, to ask that a child wait until the other children at the table have finished.

KIDS ADD EASY ELEGANCE TO ANY JELLY GLASS WITH THE BIRD O' PARADISE NAPKIN FOLD

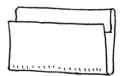

1. Fold with overlap

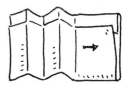

2. Fold in creases 1½" wide

3. Clip pleats at bottom, place in glass and fan out

65

COMMON INFRINGEMENTS OF ETIQUETTE MADE BY CHILDREN. LET'S AVOID THEM.

COMMON INFRINGEMENTS OF ETIQUETTE (CONTINUED, UNFORTUNATELY)

How to Build a Gingerbread House

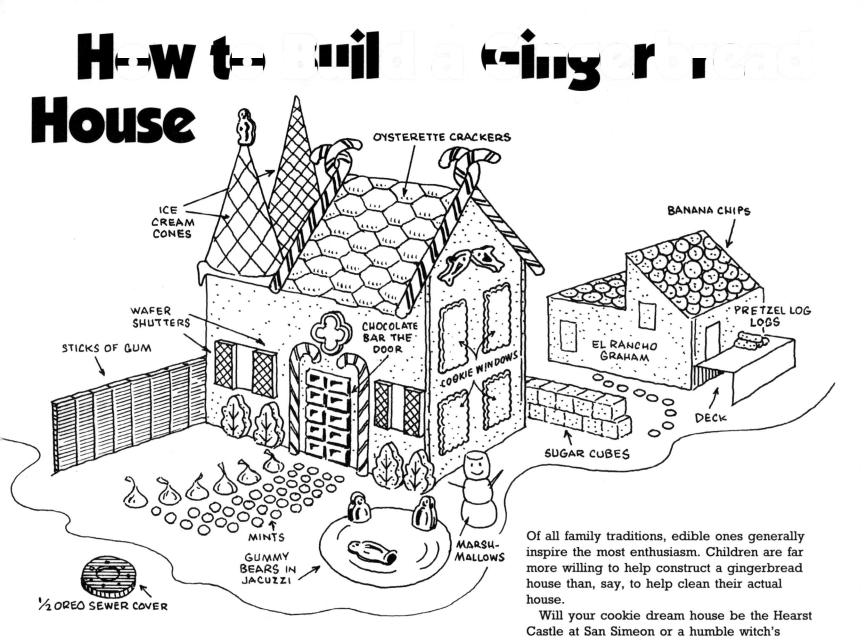

ICE CREAM CONES

OYSTERETTE CRACKERS

BANANA CHIPS

WAFER SHUTTERS

PRETZEL LOG LOGS

STICKS OF GUM

CHOCOLATE BAR THE DOOR

COOKIE WINDOWS

EL RANCHO GRAHAM

DECK

SUGAR CUBES

MINTS

GUMMY BEARS IN JACUZZI

MARSH-MALLOWS

½ OREO SEWER COVER

Of all family traditions, edible ones generally inspire the most enthusiasm. Children are far more willing to help construct a gingerbread house than, say, to help clean their actual house.

Will your cookie dream house be the Hearst Castle at San Simeon or a humble witch's cottage? Will it be Prairie style or postmodern?

You may make your plans before shopping for building materials or go directly to the supermarket for inspiration. A shopping expedition that is limited to the cookie, candy, and cereal aisles is one that most children will enjoy. Consider the structural possibilities of every item. For example:

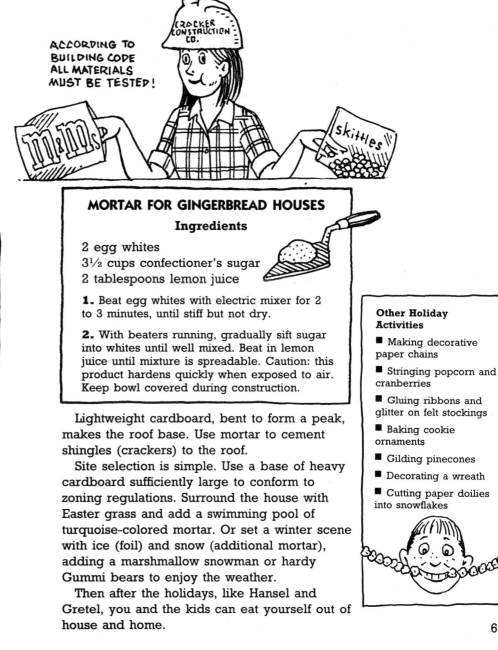

ACCORDING TO BUILDING CODE ALL MATERIALS MUST BE TESTED!

CRACKER CONSTRUCTION CO.

m&m's   skittles

> Yogurt-covered raisins = fieldstones
> Necco wafers (licorice) = slate paving
> Wheat Chex = thatched roof
> Spearmint leaves = fir trees
> Pretzel rods = wooden logs
> Sugar cubes = glass bricks

Sampling the purchased materials is of course required, in conformance with building codes.

In the past, gingerbread housing involved actual sheets of gingerbread, but their essentially fragile nature turned many an aspiring architect into Frank Lloyd Wrong. That is why sturdy, prefab graham crackers have become the drywall of postwar baked building construction. In fact, "gingerbread" Levittowns have even been constructed using the top third of milk or juice cartons (the sloping sides make a pitched roof, and if a plastic pour spout exists, it can be covered in cardboard and turned into a chimney).

MORTAR FOR GINGERBREAD HOUSES

Ingredients

2 egg whites
3½ cups confectioner's sugar
2 tablespoons lemon juice

1. Beat egg whites with electric mixer for 2 to 3 minutes, until stiff but not dry.

2. With beaters running, gradually sift sugar into whites until well mixed. Beat in lemon juice until mixture is spreadable. Caution: this product hardens quickly when exposed to air. Keep bowl covered during construction.

Lightweight cardboard, bent to form a peak, makes the roof base. Use mortar to cement shingles (crackers) to the roof.

Site selection is simple. Use a base of heavy cardboard sufficiently large to conform to zoning regulations. Surround the house with Easter grass and add a swimming pool of turquoise-colored mortar. Or set a winter scene with ice (foil) and snow (additional mortar), adding a marshmallow snowman or hardy Gummi bears to enjoy the weather.

Then after the holidays, like Hansel and Gretel, you and the kids can eat yourself out of house and home.

Other Holiday Activities

■ Making decorative paper chains

■ Stringing popcorn and cranberries

■ Gluing ribbons and glitter on felt stockings

■ Baking cookie ornaments

■ Gilding pinecones

■ Decorating a wreath

■ Cutting paper doilies into snowflakes

How to Play Hopscotch

The one sport in which city children might have a competitive edge is hopscotch, for the essential ingredient is pavement, not always available in bucolic settings.

Your child will also need chalk, a marker (a stone or shell in the country, perhaps a bottlecap or subway token in the city), and at least one other player.

Draw the playing field with chalk, then choose turns.

First player stands below the bottom line and tosses a marker into space 1. If it lands inside the lines, hop into the next box. When there are two spaces side by side, player jumps with one foot in each. For single spaces, player hops.

So first player:

- Tosses marker into space 1
- Hops into space 2
- Hops into space 3
- Jumps into spaces 4/5
- Hops into space 6
- Jumps into spaces 7/8

- Turns and lands again in spaces 7/8, facing toward space 1
- Retraces pattern, pausing to bend over and pick up the marker in space 1

Other players take a turn. Then first player throws the marker into space 2 and repeats the hopping and jumping sequence, beginning with a hop into space 1.

If your marker lands outside the numbered box or on a line, turn passes to the next player.

If you stumble your turn ends and you start with the same number on your next turn. For example, if you trip as you are returning to get the marker from space 3, you must repeat the number 3 pattern on your next turn.

First player to go through all the spaces wins.

Variations:

- Make a playing field of different shapes (see illustration).
- Add rest spaces, into which you can jump with both feet.
- Jump into the space in which the marker is thrown.

- When a player has a successful turn, player can initial space in which the marker is resting. No one else can step in the space, but the person who "owns" it can stand in it.

71

How to Watch a Game

MY BABY!
MY BABY!

Before consciousnesses were raised, sports were primarily a dad/son thing. But today boys and girls are equally likely to participate in all sorts of athletics and mom is expected to be in the stands cheering on her young athlete.

Each season brings a different game and sometimes several. You should at least know the name of the position your child is playing and it would be nice to have some understanding of the game. But what really counts is knowing the rules of *watching*. Fortunately, these are the same for every game, no matter how many players are involved and whether it is played on a court, track, or field.

1. Keep your eyes on the action. A child who has just made a remarkable play or is simply contemplating one will be very deflated if a peek into the stands reveals mom checking her lipstick or admiring her neighbor's snapshots. It is okay to chat so long as your eye motions suggest that you are watching the play.

2. Cheer loudly, but no louder than anyone else. Although the notion of ''sportsmanship'' is thrown around by people trying to drum up financial support for athletic programs, your child will interpret restraint as lack of interest. It may seem indecorous to make noise in order to distract the competition during a critical moment, boo the competition and hoot at the ref, but that's how you show support. However, don't make so much noise that you make a spectacle of yourself.

3. Root for the correct team. Very important concept. Though as a goodwill gesture, you will probably be forgiven for cheering a terrific play by a friend's child on the opposing team, rooting for the other side out of ignorance or confusion is a humiliating error. Make sure you know the color of your child's team uniform or jersey and which goal, basket, or whatever your child's team is shooting for. (Remember that in basketball, the teams change sides at the half.)

4. Let the coach handle injuries. While you will find it practically irresistible to rush to your child's side immediately, wait a few minutes. Excessive mommish concern is humiliating, particularly to a boy. The situation is almost inevitably less grave than it initially appears. Many a young athlete who is writhing on the ground one minute is begging to be returned to play the next.

5. Stay attentive for the replay. Following the game, your child will rehash the highlights and low moments of the game in a long, drawn-out (as opposed to instant) replay. Even if you understand practically nothing, if you listen closely your mom instinct will kick in so you'll know when to nod sympathetically and when to become indignant. Even if the team went down in flames, your child may have had a personally satisfying game. Well, it's theoretically possible.

6. Bring refreshments.

How to Lead a Cheer

MOVING THE ARMS

Hands should be held straight out from the wrist, folded into a fist, or curled as if holding a stick. The following arm movements will help rouse the crowd. (In each case, when using only one arm, keep the other on your hip.)

- Hand on Hip.
- Wide Reach. Arm held straight out wide.
- Shoulder Reach. Arm is bent and reaching toward opposite shoulder.
- Chest Pounder. Arm is bent and hand held over collar bone.
- High or Low V. Arm pointed at 45 degree angle up or down.
- High or Low Reach. Arm reaches straight up or down.

MOVING THE FEET

Legs should be kept together. Bounce from one foot to the other, alternately pointing the toe and planting the foot on the ground.

At the end of the cheer a jump is always appropriate. Variations on the basic jump include:

Everyone can use a cheering session now and then—to celebrate a triumph, to climb out of a funk, or just for the fun of it. If you can show your child how to do a cartwheel and/or a split, you will get extra respect. But enthusiasm alone counts for a lot. (And a pompon or two won't hurt.)

74

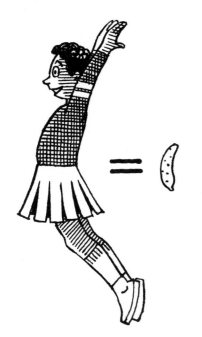

The banana. When this is done correctly, the body viewed from the side appears to be curved like a banana.

Spread-eagle. Start with legs and arms straight down, then do a jumping jack in the air.

The tuck. Knees are brought up to chest and "hugged" in midair. Arms are spread in a high V as feet return to earth.

The Herkie. Named after H. L. Herkimer, founder of the National Cheerleaders Association, this has several variations. In the basic Herkie, in midair one leg is pointed straight out to the side and the other is bent.

A Simple Cheer (Including Choreography)

Begin by standing at attention: feet together, body pointed forward, eyes looking straight ahead, arms hanging straight down, palms on thighs.

Words WORK-		ING		TO BE	THE	BEST!
Movements Two-arm chest pound	Clap	Two-arm Low V	Clap	Two-arm High Reach	Clap	One-arm High V

ALL THAT One Shoulder Reach	YOU CAN Other Shoulder Reach	BE! Two-arm High V	PROVE IT One hand on hip	MOVE IT Other hand on hip	M-O-V-E! Cup arms around mouth and shout out letters	Jump!

OTHER CHEERS

Come on (clap) crowd (clap)
Yell it loud! (clap)
Give us a(n) (First Letter of name of child)
Give us a(n) (Second letter of name of child)
(Continue until name is spelled out)
Put it all together; what've you got?
(Yell each letter, following each with a clap)
YAY!

Two bits, four bits, six bits, a dollar
All for (name of child), stand up and holler!
YAY!

Hey-hey-hey!
What d'ya say!
Everything will go your way!

Hey, (clap) (clap) (name of child)
We're rootin' for you!
So hey, (clap) (clap) (name of child)
Pull through!

Hoo-ray for (name of child)!
Hoo-ray for (name of child)!
Someone in the crowd is yelling "Hoo-ray for
(name of child)!"
One—Two—Three—Four!
Who do you think we're rooting for?
(Name of child), that's who.

North—South—East—West!
(Name of child) is the very (clap hands twice)
best!

Catch a big lion,
Put him in the ka-bah!
Lion in the da-bah!
Bim! Boom! Bee! Baa Baa!
Ish Noo Whitney Atten Batten
Bow Bow Ski Watten Datten
Boom! Chow! Boom! Chow!

How to Turn Ten Plastic Grocery Bags into a Pompom

1. Stack bags, handles all pointing in the same direction.
2. Flatten them to remove air.

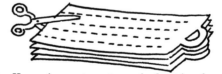

3. Use scissors to cut one-inch strips from bottom almost to top of bag. Do not cut handles.

4. Loop yarn through bag handles and tie tightly at top.
5. Loop a second piece of yarn around base of bag handles and tie tightly.

2-4-6-8!
SHOPPING BAGS
ARE REALLY
GREAT!

How to Make Paper Dolls

TRAGEDY STRIKES!

It takes talent to be a "paper engineer" who designs pop-up books that are practically animated, an origami master who can turn a single piece of paper into a zooful of creatures, or a commuter who can fold a newspaper so it can be read on a subway during rush hour. But even if you've never managed anything more complicated than making a paper napkin into a triangle, you can teach your child how to cut paper dolls.

PAPER DOLLS

Fold paper accordian style. Starting from the top of the fold, draw half a figure. Give it a flip hairdo and a skirt. Cut around the figure and unfold the paper.

Important to remember: One element of the figure must reach clear across the page to the edge. It may be the arm and hand or even the hem of the skirt. If you have not done this properly, you will not have a chain of paper dolls, you will have a stack of paper dolls.

PAPER GUYS

Proceed as above but design figure with short hair and pant legs.

PAPER GUYS AND DOLLS

Fold paper accordian style and draw half a female figure on one fold and half a male figure on the other, holding hands.

PAPER GUYS AND DOLLS IN THE STYLE OF PICASSO

Make random cuts in the folded paper strip and say that whatever comes out is your impression of a human figure.

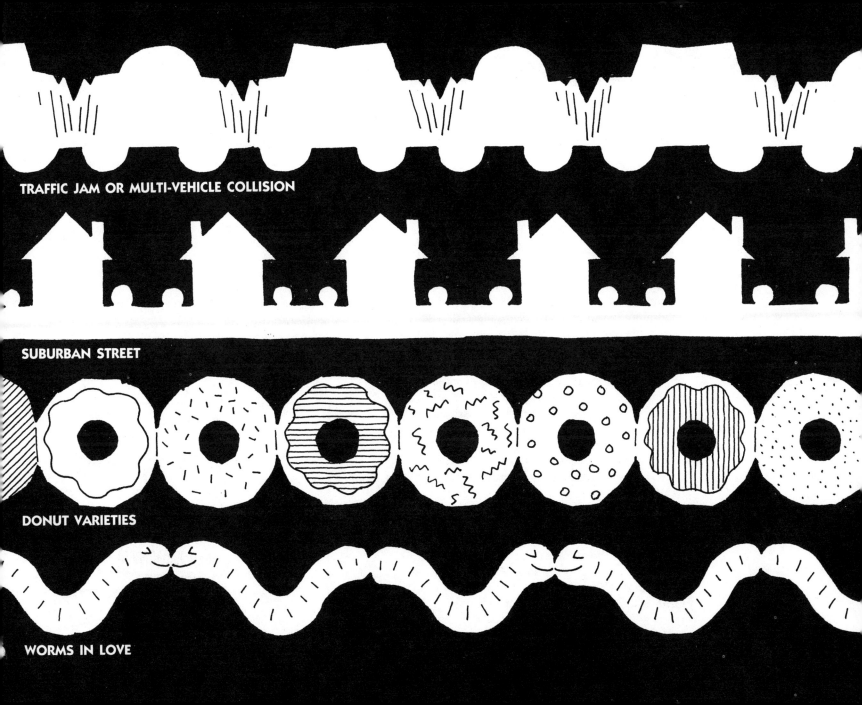

TRAFFIC JAM OR MULTI-VEHICLE COLLISION

SUBURBAN STREET

DONUT VARIETIES

WORMS IN LOVE

How to Wash Up

CHILD'S HAND BEFORE WASHING BY CHILD

CHILD'S HAND AFTER WASHING BY CHILD

Though many animals are born knowing how to groom themselves, the complexity of human grooming requires years of training. It is only over time that children learn to navigate the shoals of hair conditioner and dental floss.

Little girls are generally more pliant than little boys about responding to requests about personal care, though the invention of the water-resistant portable radio has had a dramatic effect on the amount of time preteen boys are willing to spend in the shower. In any event, once adolescence kicks in, this department takes care of itself. Until then, Mom has to lead the way.

WASHING HANDS

Studies have shown that the average child responds to the phrase "Wash your hands before you come to the table!" only after 5.4 repetitions. When the child shows up at the table ask, "Did you wash your hands?" because a visual inspection does not always yield the answer. You should also ask, "Did you use soap?"

BRUSHING AND COMBING HAIR

Removing snarls, the occupational hazard of having long hair, is so emotionally exhausting that some children are tempted merely to stop brushing altogether. But this merely increases snarl incidence and also promotes the loss of objects in the hair.

Boys, whose heads are generally covered by baseball caps, may argue that combing or brushing serves no purpose and they may have a point.

Some boys and girls may find brushing preferable to combing. In any event, cheap plastic combs with sharp teeth should never be used on children. They are, however, excellent for shredding cheese.

BRUSHING TEETH

Your dentist, using colorfully illustrated visual aids to explain the horrific consequences of allowing bacteria to go about their work undisturbed, can probably make the most persuasive argument for brushing teeth. Nowadays, in a classic example of the mixed-message concept, children's toothpastes and mouthwashes come flavored like the very foods we tell them not to eat because they are bad for the teeth.

No child understands the necessity for brushing in the morning.

New York children's dentist Dr. Ken Markel offers this guide to toothbrushing:

1. Clean a baby's gums with a warm washcloth as soon as first teeth appear.

2. Begin toothbrushing when baby has several teeth (ages 3–18 months) using a soft toothbrush and a very tiny amount of toothpaste, since the child is too young to spit it out.

3. Once a child asks to "do it myself," encourage it, twice a day. Mom should go over the evening toothbrushing "to make sure it is perfect" until child is 7 or 8 and can do it properly.

4. Explain that only a small amount of toothpaste is necessary. The direction of the brush is not important but being gentle and thorough is. Pay special attention to all chewing surfaces, the rear of the mouth, and along the inside and outside gumlines.

5. When the bristles are bent and/or frayed, the brush should be replaced.

H--w t-- M-k-- a B-d

If your child will be going away to school or camp or has plans to join the military, having mastered the art of bedmaking will be a real feather in his or her cap. If your child is an overnight guest, bedmaking may also score points with the hostess, though it is no substitute for bringing a house gift.

BEDMAKING FOR BEGINNERS

As many a child has discovered at camp—where the practice is more likely to be tolerated—if you lie in your sleeping bag on top of your bed, you do not have to make the bed at all.

VERY CAREFULLY SLIP OUT OF THE ENVELOPE.

But even when your child has slept under the covers, if no scary dream caused him or her to thrash around, he or she may be able to slip out very, very carefully, and the bed will look made simply by smoothing down the blanket and plumping up the pillow.

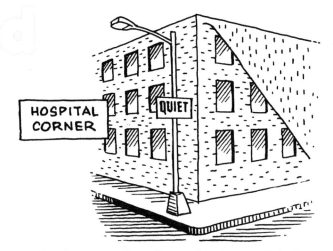

HOSPITAL CORNER

QUIET

To plump up the pillow, give it a sock in the middle, then grab it by the edges and shake it. Foam pillows don't need plumping, as they resume their original shape even when run over by a Mack truck. Still, even if it does nothing for the pillow, plumping is a good way to release hostile feelings.

ADVANCED BEDMAKING

The bottom layer is the fitted sheet.

The next layer is the flat or top sheet. The big hem goes at the top of the bed. Lay it down about 1 inch from the headboard. Tuck in hospital corners (see below). If you are using a blanket, you can make the hospital corners with blanket and top sheet together.

The top layer is the quilt or comforter.

Finally, put new pillowcases on the pillows and put them back in place.

Some people put a bedspread on top of everything.

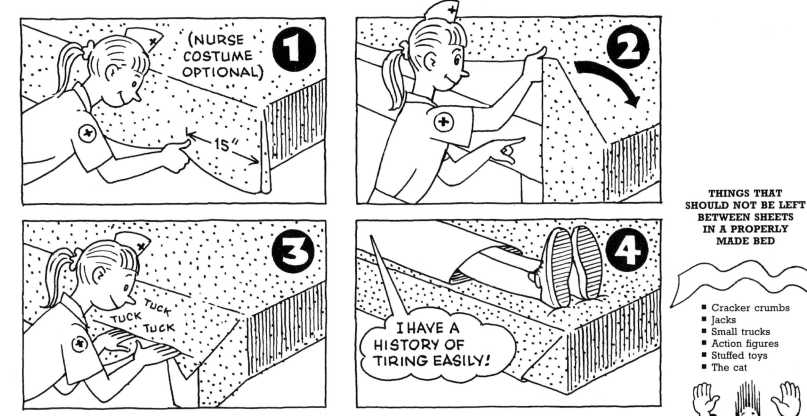

THINGS THAT SHOULD NOT BE LEFT BETWEEN SHEETS IN A PROPERLY MADE BED

- Cracker crumbs
- Jacks
- Small trucks
- Action figures
- Stuffed toys
- The cat

HOSPITAL CORNER

To make a hospital corner, pick up the edge of the sheet (and if you are using a blanket, the blanket also) about 15 inches from the foot of the bed. Lift it up so it makes a diagonal fold. Lay the fold on the mattress. Take the part of the sheet (and blanket) that is hanging and tuck it underneath the mattress. Drop the fold, pull it smooth, and tuck it under the mattress too.

A hospital corner is not a pharmaceutical or medical term. It is derived from hospital bedmaking. The best bedmakers in the world are nurses, who, in a series of complex turns and flips, are able to make beds even while people are in them. This is advanced professional bedmaking and not recommended for your child at home.

How to Put on a Puppet Show

KIDS CAN MAKE:

Tickets

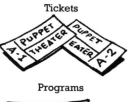

Programs

Posters

Once Punch could throw his weight around with only Judy to challenge him. Nowadays the two of them must compete with the electronic whammy of Game Boy® and similar entertainments to engage the attention of children. Still, "homemade" entertainment such as a puppet play continues to have enormous appeal. Creating their own shows is a natural outlet for children's inventiveness. Besides, being generally controlled by larger persons, children enjoy the opportunity to dominate other creatures even smaller than themselves.

There are puppets with more strings than a stalk of celery. Mastering these complex marionettes takes years. The true hand puppet, however, can be animated in moments with nothing more than couple of marking pens and some imagination.

PUTTING A MOUTH IN YOUR FOOT

Of all constructed puppets, the sock puppet is the easiest to make. The puppet will have a working mouth, so big-mouthed characters like

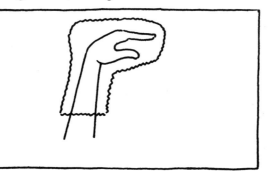

alligators, dimetrodons, or political extremists are within the realm of possibilities.

Any old sock will do, but a colored sock may suit (or suggest) a particular character. You will also need hot glue or white glue and markers; felt triangles, buttons, and other craft odds and ends will also come in handy.

To make the mouth, fold a piece of lightweight cardboard and cut half an oval. Open the oval cutout and use a marker to color it red. Wedge it into the toe area of the sock and glue it in place.

Your child makes the mouth move by putting four fingers above and the thumb below the cardboard insert.

Draw eyes with markers. Or glue on buttons or the rolling eyes found in craft stores.

Use markers or felt bits to add character

details such as arched eyebrows, flaring nostrils, or two days' growth of stubble. Add bandages or a necklace or bowtie.

Make hair or a mane by gluing on yarn.

Felt triangles can make ears or a reptile's back.

A forked tongue or tooth will make the sock saurian.

ALL THE WORLD'S A CARTON

Tape a medium-sized cardboard carton closed and make four openings:

1. A slot to hold scenery at the rear of the stage

2. A small slot for the curtain

3. A proscenium arch

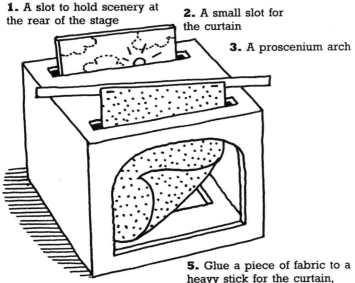

4. A rectangle at the bottom for the puppets to come through

5. Glue a piece of fabric to a heavy stick for the curtain, which is a necessity. No child has the complete impresario experience without having said, "Curtain going up!"

PLOTS AND PLAYS

Unless you've made the stage from the carton your stove came in, four characters onstage (two puppeteers, each using two hands) is the max your facility can handle. Think "Goldilocks and the Three Bears" rather than *Les Miserables*. The possibilities for a one-person show include (but are not limited to) the Weather Channel and "Snow White and the One Dwarf."

I DON'T DO WINDOWS.

TONITE!! SOCK WHITE AND THE ONE DWARF

FLASHLIGHT SPOTLIGHT

Fold cardboard for furniture

GLUE

85

How to Plié

Perhaps if "plié" were pronounced "ply," as if it were somehow connected to pliers, it would interest more boys. But *plié* (pronounced plee-AY), a French word that means "to bend," is a ballet term. And though nowadays many little girls are willing to pitch in a Little League game, few boys are interested in pliéing in a production of Swan Lake.

Ballet is a good learning experience that can teach your child how to follow instructions, keep a straight back, and apply bright blue eye shadow. It teaches you to sharpen your powers of observation so you can distinguish your child from the forty-nine other mice crowding the stage in the ballet school's production of the *Nutcracker*.

When your child expresses interest in joining the troupe of Madame Fallingova, you can introduce some of the basics right at home.

WARMING UP

Like a car, a ballerina should never start cold. Your child can warm up with these simple exercises.

Knee Bounces. Sit on the floor, bottoms of feet together and knees part. Gently bounce knees toward the floor. Repeat 7 times.

Head Bounces. Relax the knees and loosely bounce the head toward the knees. Repeat 7 times. Gently.

Stretches. Stretch up and reach toward the ceiling, arms and back straight. Repeat 7 times.

Curves. Gently drop the head toward the feet, keeping the back round, counting to eight. Repeat twice.

THE POSITIONS OF THE FEET

Ballet choreography is based on five positions of the feet. The first three are very easy but the fourth position and fifth position are tricky.

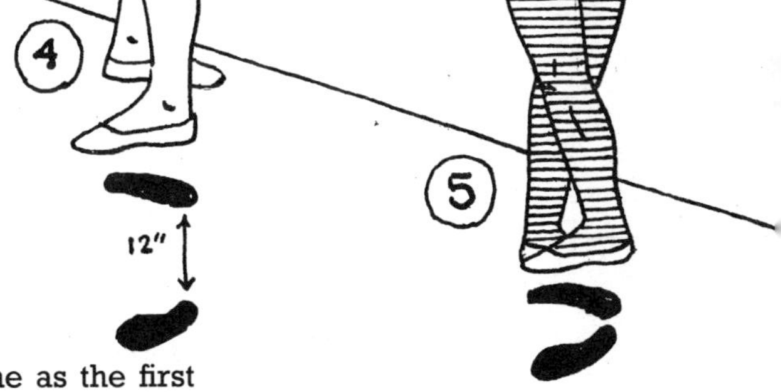

First Position. Put the heels together and turn the feet and legs out as far as the thighs can turn *without forcing.*

Second Position. Turn the thighs outward again with feet placed one to one and a half foot lengths apart.

Third Position. Put the heel of one foot against the middle of the other foot. Turn both feet out.

Fourth Position. Same as the first position but with one foot about twelve inches forward of the other.

Fifth Position. Turn both feet out, just as in first position, but place the heel of one foot against the toes of the other. This is not easy.

FOOT ← POSITION

12"

87

FIRST STEPS

These three steps, based on the positions, can be turned into a dance. They may also be your child's first French lesson. Before you know it, you may catch her asking for a *grand* order of *pommes frittes* at the CharBurger.

Bourée (boo-RAY). With feet together, stand on demi-point (dem-mee PWA), which means on half-pointed foot—in other words, on the balls of the feet. Take a small, sliding step forward. Repeat with the other foot. When this step is executed properly, your daughter will look as if she's wearing high heels and a short, tight shirt.

Sauter (sew-TAY). From the first position, go into a demi-plié (half-bend) and jump high in the air. Land in a demi-plié and lower the heels gently to the floor.

Point (PWA). Place the foot in the third position. Point the right foot and slide it out about 8 inches at a 45-degree angle.

A DANCE

Roll back the rug, put on some music, and put the three steps together.

The steps and music should end together. That is when the applause should begin. When the applause ends, your child may curtsy.

BOUREÉ 20 TIMES

SAUTER 6 TIMES

POINT 10 TIMES

DOWNSTAIRS NEIGHBOR STARTS COMPLAINING HERE

WHAT'S GOING ON UP THERE?

IT'S THAT KID AGAIN, SHE SOUNDS LIKE A HERD OF ELEPHANTS.

How to Make a Ballerina's Bun
First, have your daughter grow her hair as long as possible. (If hair is also straight and very fine, that is helpful.) Then, gather it at the nape of the neck into a pony tail, holding it with an elastic band. Twist the pony tail and coil it tightly around. Secure it with bobby pins.

PULLING EFFECT OF TOO-TIGHT BUN

HOW TO CURTSY

Imagine a clock on the floor. Your child is in the center, facing 12. Her feet are in the third position, right foot ahead of left. She bends her knees in a demi-plié and slides her right foot along the floor to 12 o'clock. Then she rotates it around the dial to 7 o'clock. She bends her knees a little further and bows her head to observe the growing pile of bouquets thrown at her feet.

How to Make Believe

Children don't need much help to play at make believe. They just need you to turn off the TV and perhaps provide sources of inspiration: old clothes to dress up in; large boxes to play inside; tables to hide under; blankets to make a cave. Even an ordinary chair can be transformed with a little imagination.

How to Say Goodnight

The rituals associated with bedtime are among the sweetest of parenting experiences. This is more likely to be so when the child is pleasantly tired rather than crankily exhausted.

Do not postpone bedtime until your child is about to fall over in a stupor. (Some people consider this "natural" childrearing. However, in a truly natural environment, the child is lulled to sleep when darkness falls rather than while watching late-night talk shows.)

And resist the urge to prolong, add to, and complicate the tucking in rituals until they become as excessive as the Oscar ceremonies. Mom can lead a kid to quarters, and can even make him sleep. Well, anyway, you can try.

LULLABIES

Shower singers, here's your chance. Perform before a completely enthusiastic, nonjudgmental audience—and if the baby falls asleep while you're in the middle of a number, so much the better! Recordings are nice (and may teach you a few new tunes), but *your* voice singing a lullaby will be the most beautiful and soothing sound in the world to your child.

Traditional lullabies include Brahm's and "Rockabye, Baby." If you find the former hard to remember and the latter too gloomy, you can always go with the ever-popular "La-La-La-La," hummed quietly to any melody, from Presley to Puccini.

Brahm's Lullaby
Lullaby and good night; with roses bedight,
With lillies bedeck, is baby's wee bed;
Lay thee down now and rest,
May thy slumber be blest;
Lay thee down now and rest,
May thy slumber be blest.

Rockabye, Baby
Rockabye, baby, on the treetop,
When the wind blows the cradle will rock;
When the bough breaks, the cradle will fall,
And down will come baby, cradle and all.

CAUTION: THIS BEDTIME INVOCATION MAY KEEP YOUR CHILD AWAKE!

Now I lay me down to sleep, I pray the Lord my soul to keep. If I should DIE before I wake, I pray the Lord MY SOUL TO TAKE.

I JUST WANT TO FINISH THIS BOOK!

WINDING DOWN

Little children need a brief warning that bedtime is imminent. As children get older, the warning period must become longer. Anticipate the request to "just finish this television show/chapter/game" and if possible time your announcement accordingly—for example, during the third commercial break. The longer the lag time between your original request and the moment the child actually conks out, the greater the opportunity for goodwill to disintegrate. (One of the few good things about having teenagers is that their bedtime is generally later than yours so that this process is behind you.)

BEDTIME STORIES (ORIGINAL)

Some children enjoy hearing original stories, a challenge that may have inspired Lewis Carroll though perhaps not you. Bear in mind that children consider any tale thrilling if they

themselves star in it and the action involves conquering an adversary or a fear. If you are truly stumped, borrow the plot from any popular story and cast your own child in it.

BEDTIME STORIES (PUBLISHED)

For the child's sake, a bedtime read should not be scary. For the parent's sake, it should be short. Unfortunately, children eventually tire of "Goodnight Moon." On nights when you are running out of energy, it is truly okay to introduce microwave literature—stories that run two minutes or less. (If you can't find such a collection, an Aesop Fable or two will do). Books for older children tend to end each chapter with a cliffhanger so announce at the outset that the limit is one chapter per night.

MONSTER REMOVAL

Before you leave the room, a young child may request that you expel all monsters by opening up the closets, looking under the bed, and so on, and commanding them to go. If you turn an empty, re-covered air-freshener can into a "Monster Spray Remover," your child can assist you in this duty.

COMFORT EQUIPMENT

Even the most macho and mature sixth-grader may enjoy snuggling up to a fuzzy companion—especially on an overnight trip or during a stay at camp. Younger children often want a blanky or other piece of cloth and/or a pacifier. (If your child is still of pacifier age, put one in a safe place so you will not be searching underneath the crib with the flashlight in the middle of the night.)

HUGS, KISSES, PRAYERS, ET CETERA

After the story comes a hug, a kiss, maybe a prayer, and a final "I love you." Then the lights are turned out, the nightlight is switched on, and your child drifts off to dreamland. Or not. There is nothing that dispels the overwhelming love that you feel at the sight of your child sleeping peacefully in his bed as quickly as the sight of that same child in the living room, moments later, announcing that he can't sleep.

BEDTIME STORIES ARE VERY RELAXING.

H--w t-- --uild an --g--

In the boxing arena of life, there is nothing like having a mom in your corner with a towel.

A child who knows that mom is convinced of his or her greatness is invincible, at least until he or she goes to nursery school and discovers second opinions—at which point mom's reassurances will matter more than ever. Actual achievements will bolster a child's sense of accomplishment and provide a realistic yardstick for the child's own worth as he or she grows, but *only* the unabashed enthusiasm of a devoted mom can bolster a child's ego in the following ways:

Make liabilities into virtues:

"I've heard that being nearsighted is a sign of intelligence."

See the good in everything:

"So what if you threw the ball in the other team's basket? It was a perfect shot."

Seize any opportunity for praise:

"What strong wrists you have."

Be completely supportive:

"I can't think of anything that would make me happier than for you to be a stunt motorcyclist."

Promise the moon:

"Einstein wasn't good at math in school either, and look how he turned out."

Give lots of hugs.

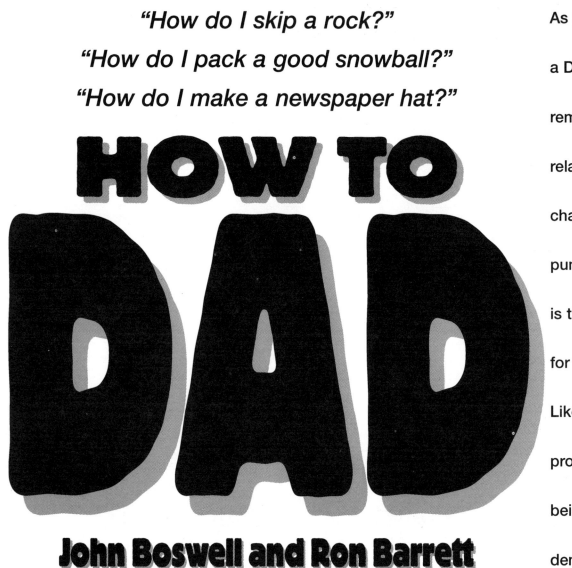